   WELCOME! We hope you enjoy this Fave Art-10 album collection of classic nude paintings. Most art works are copied from the internet, posters, pictures and books. Most are collector's items and can be seen in famous galleries and private homes. The originals are very expensive but copies are available from some dealers. You may display this book as coffee table book in your living room, as conversation piece. You may give this as gift. You may cut out and frame each page. Each art work is 8.5x11 inches and suitable for framing, and for wall decors. THANK YOU.

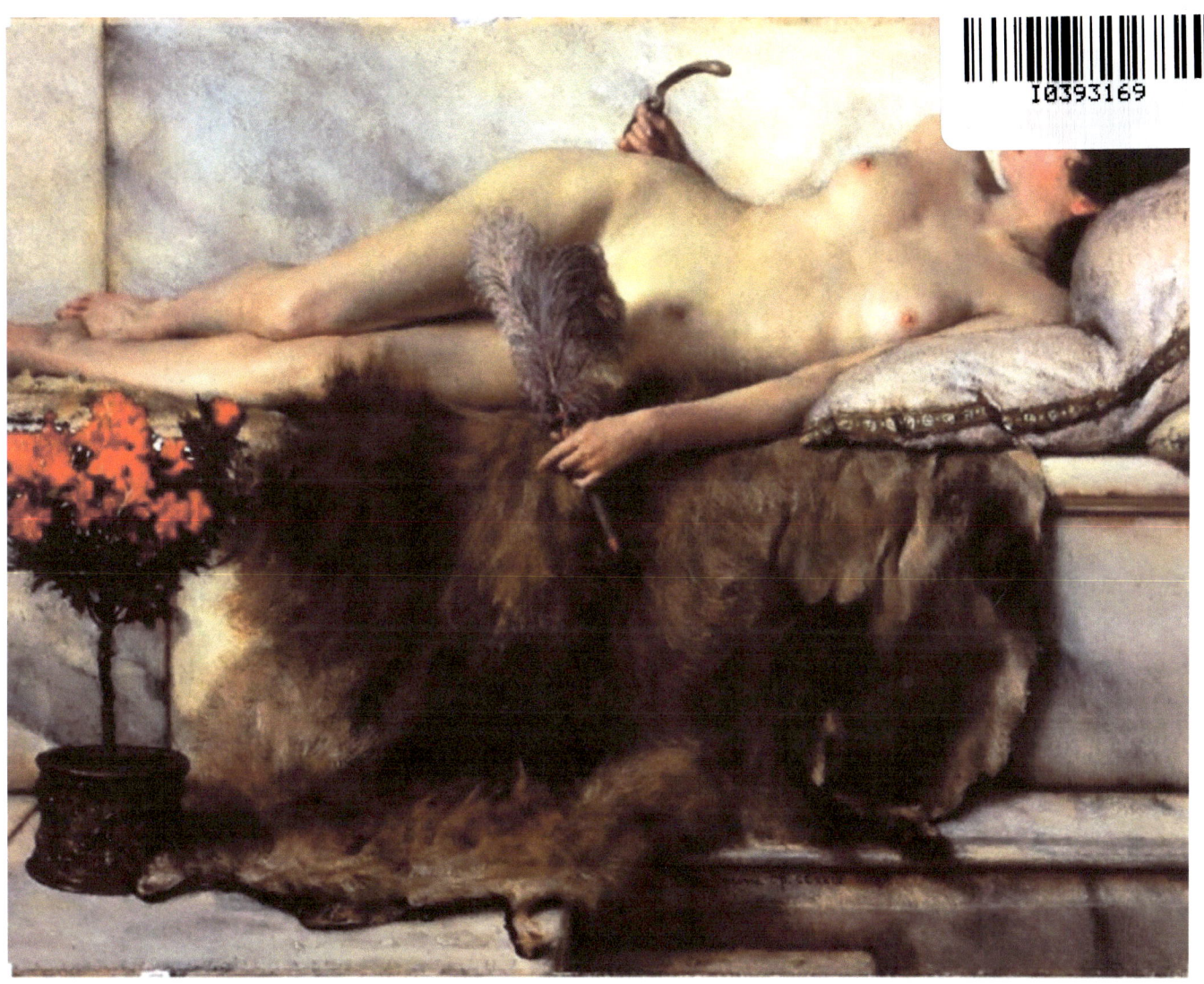

The ISBN Code Numbers of this book are:
ISBN-13: 978- 1544120898 & ISBN-10: 1544120893
Printed in USA. Free to copy by anybody. Why copy? Just buy the book.
My other books list can be accessed at:
http://tinyurl.com/mj76ccq and http://www.jobelizes6.wix.com/mysite.
My contact email is job_elizes@yahoo.com. (Tatay Jobo Elizes, Self-Pub.)

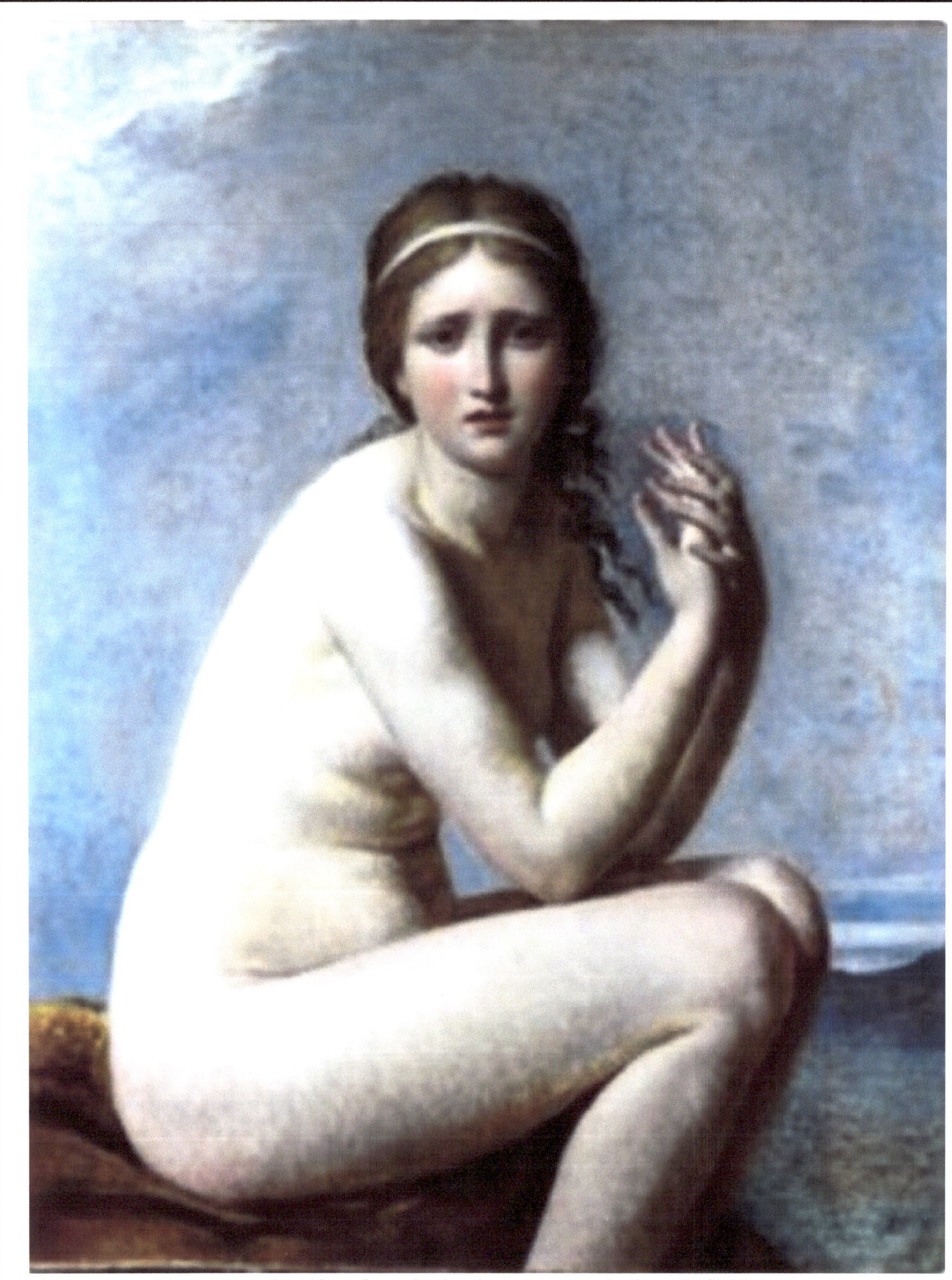

Psyche Abandoned – by Jacques Louis David, 1795

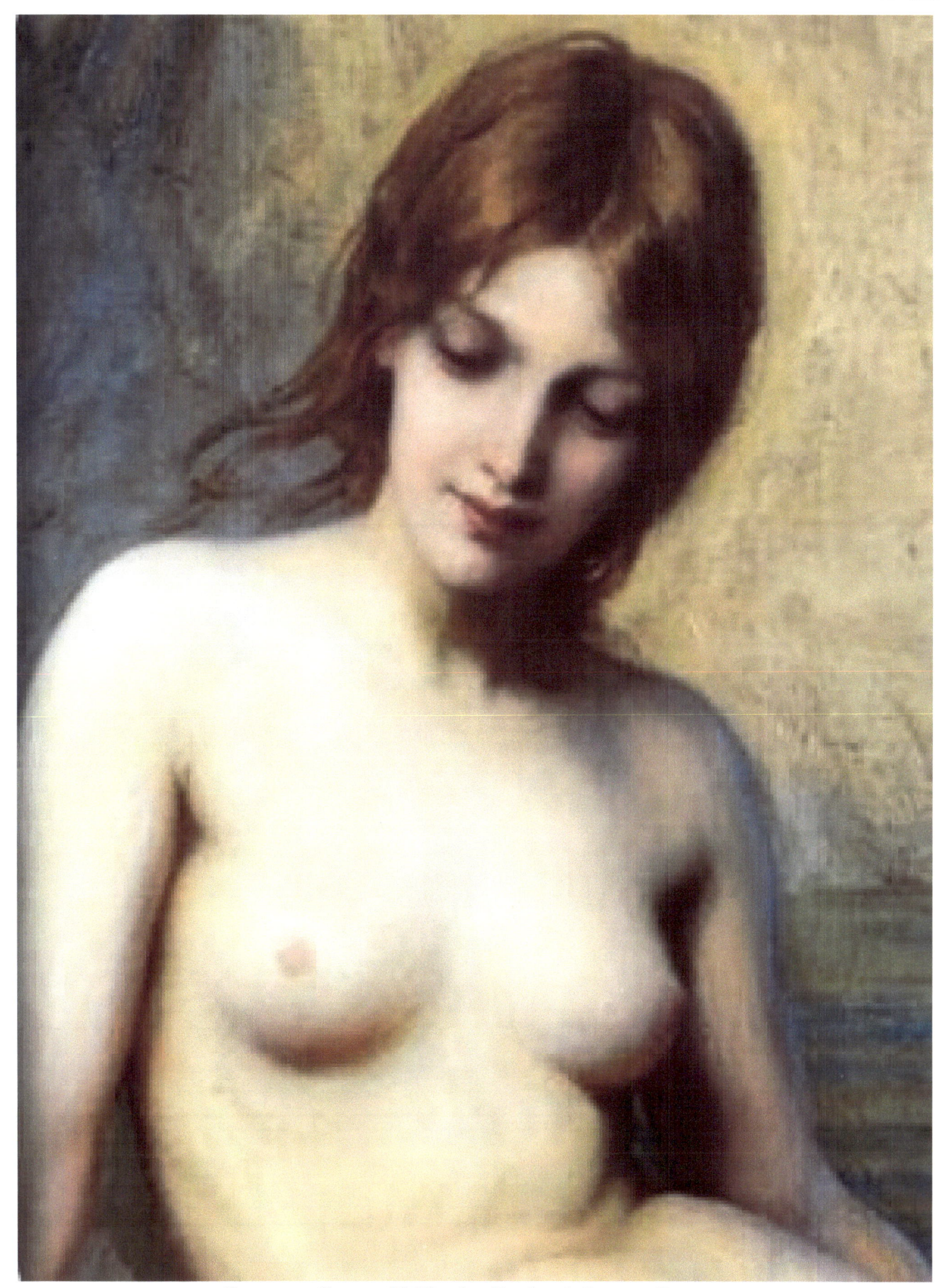

Summer Seas, 1912 – by Herbert James Draper

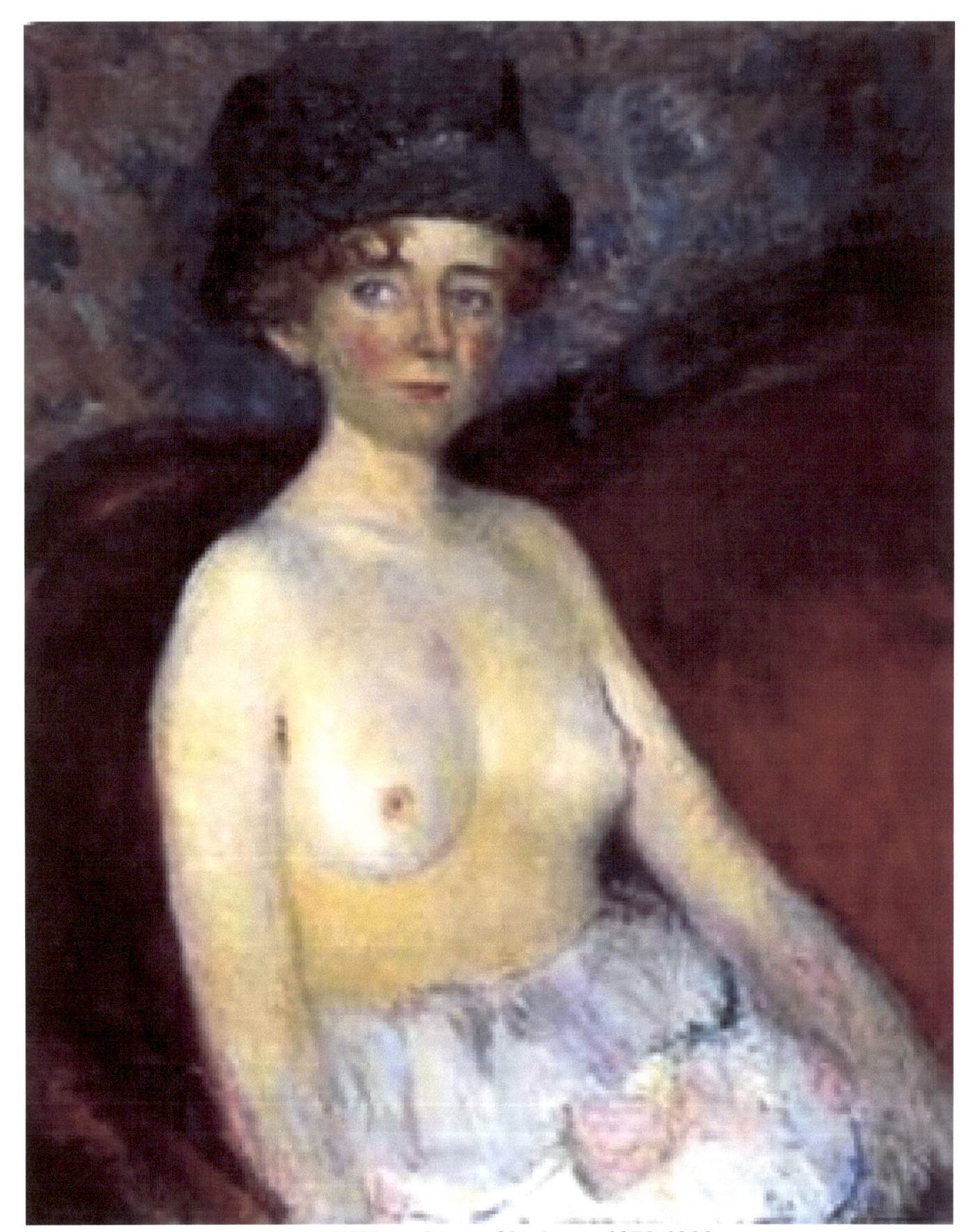

Artist – William James Glackens, 1870-1938

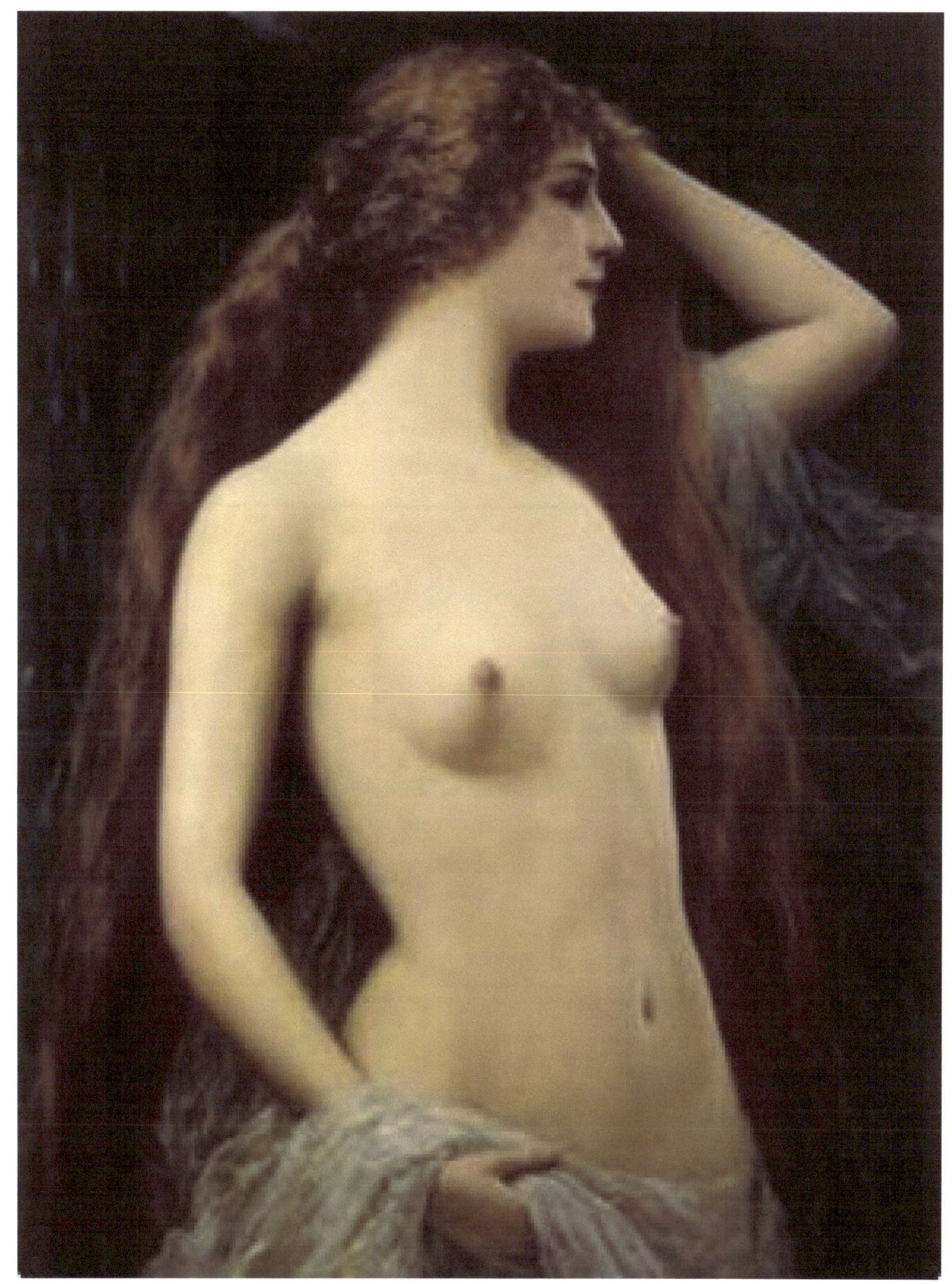

Contemplation – by Ignace Spiridon, Year Unknown

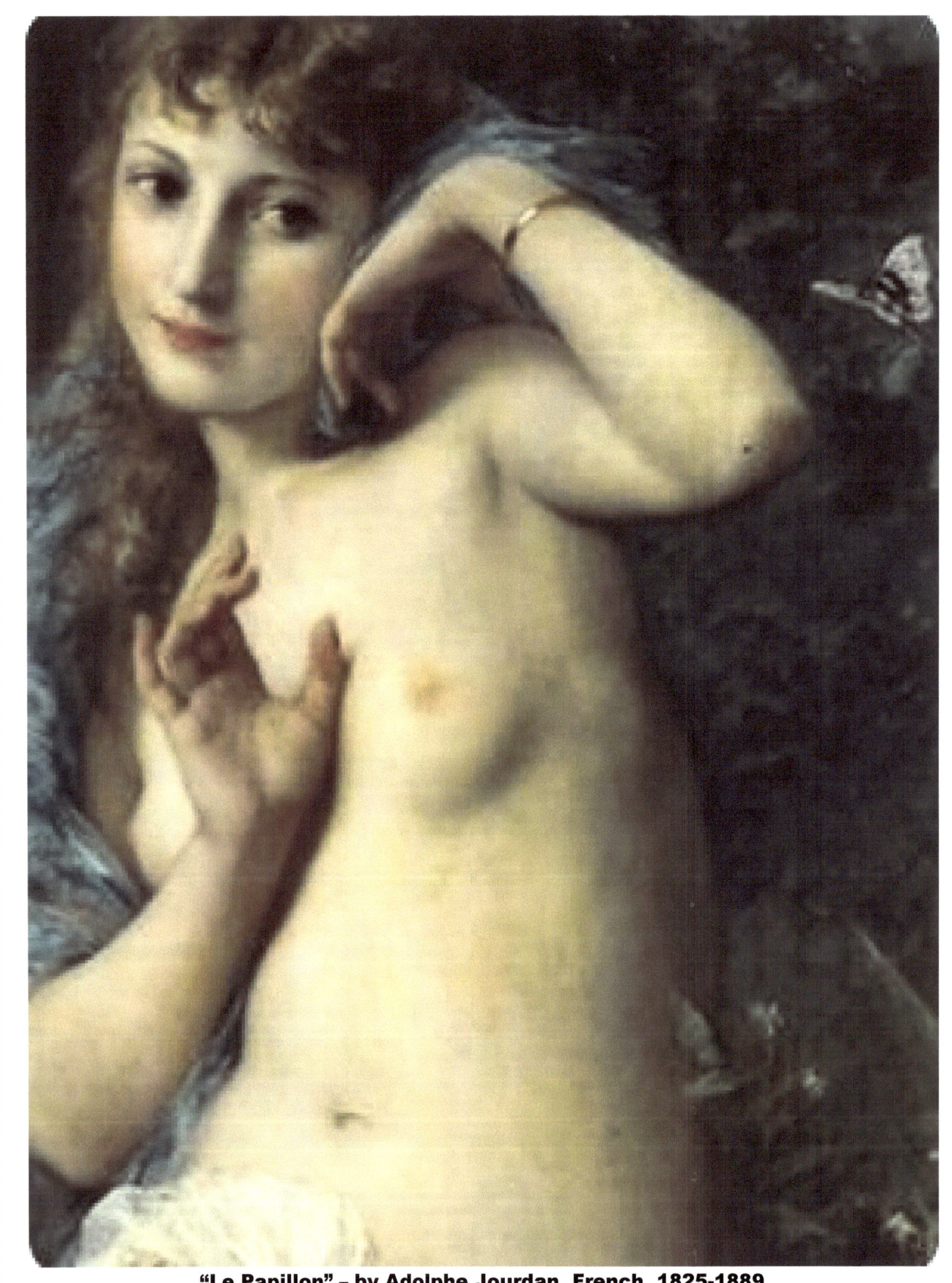

"Le Papillon" – by Adolphe Jourdan, French, 1825-1889

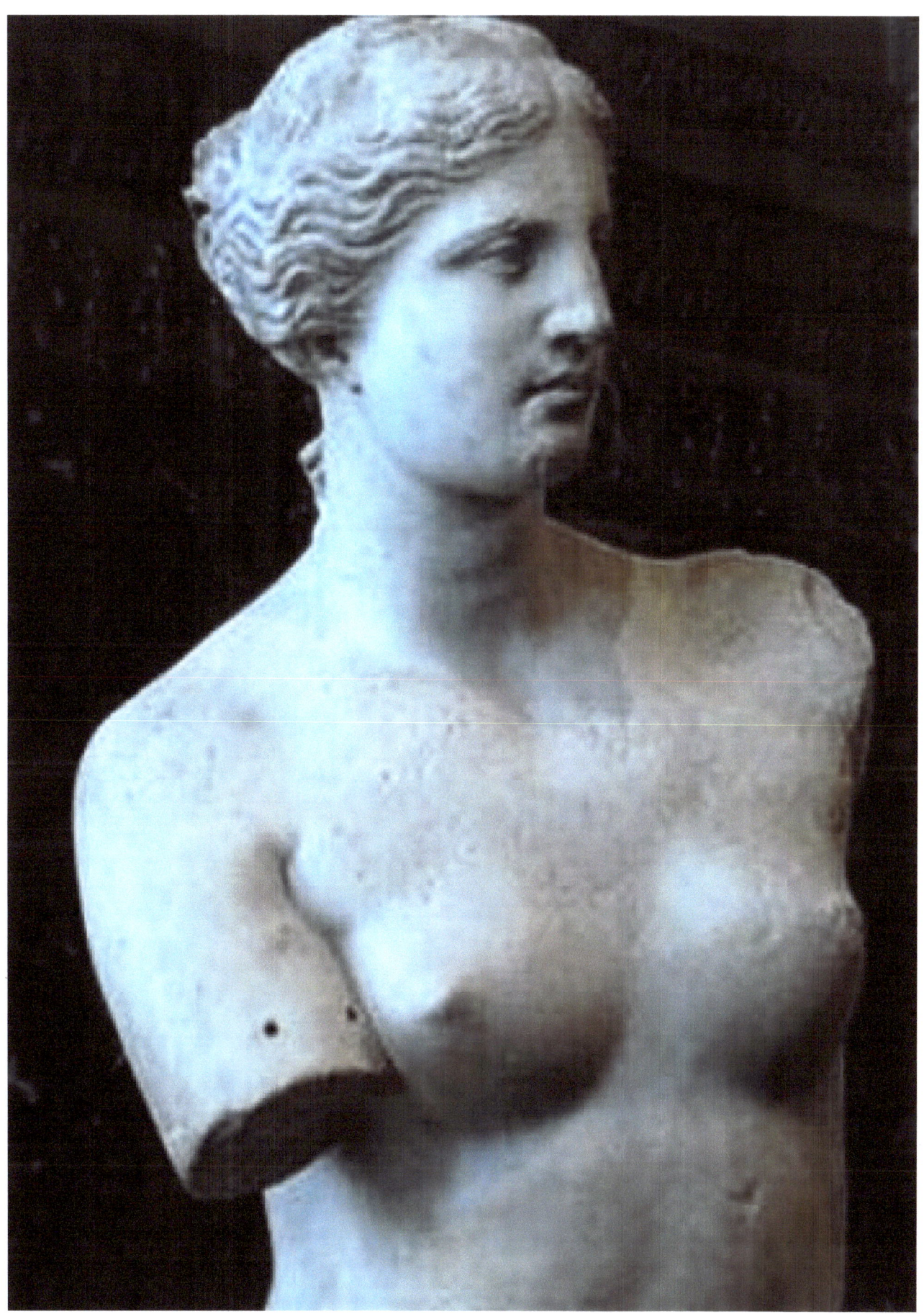

Greek Sculpture – classic features

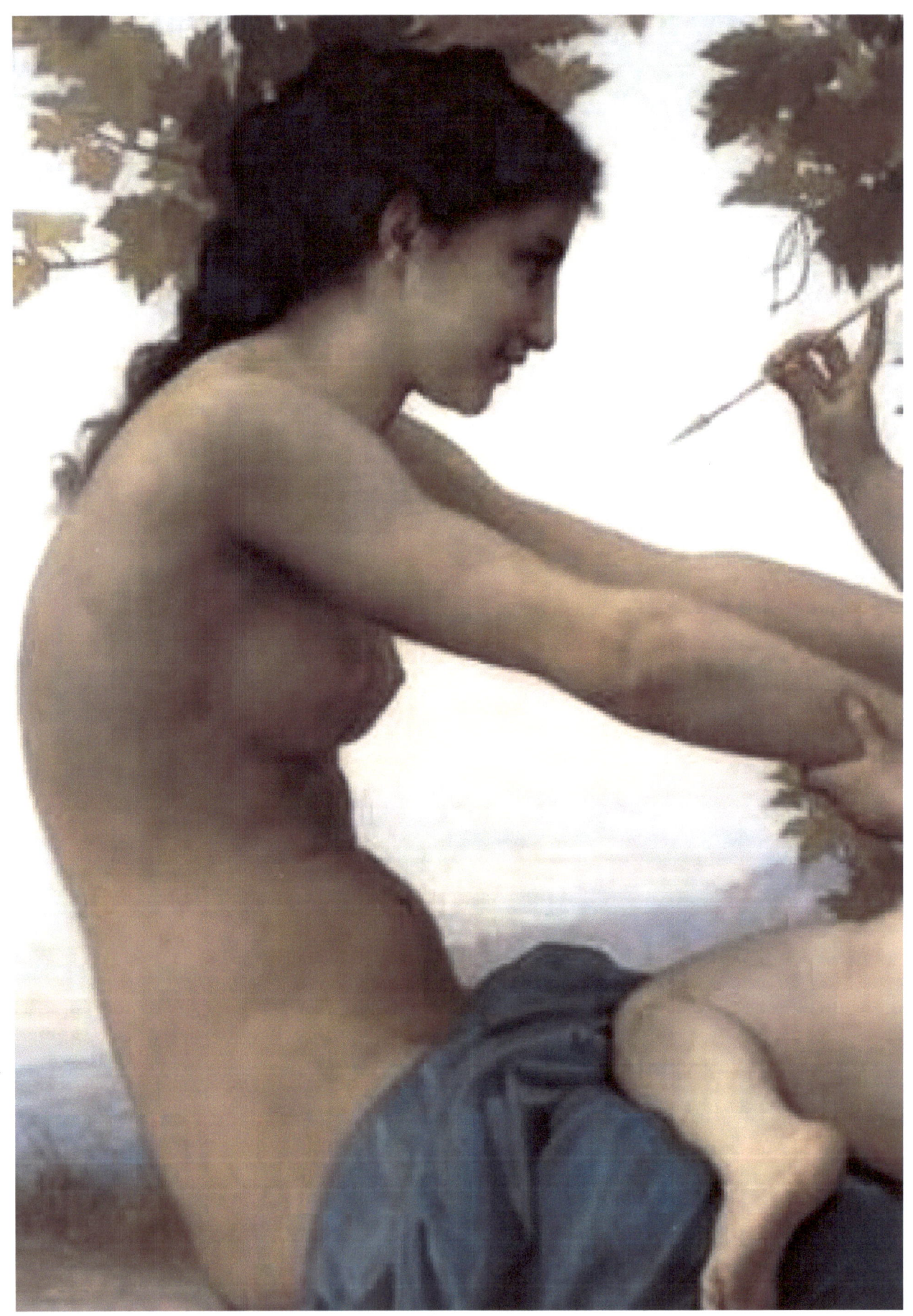

"Young girl and Eros" – Artist & Year Unknown

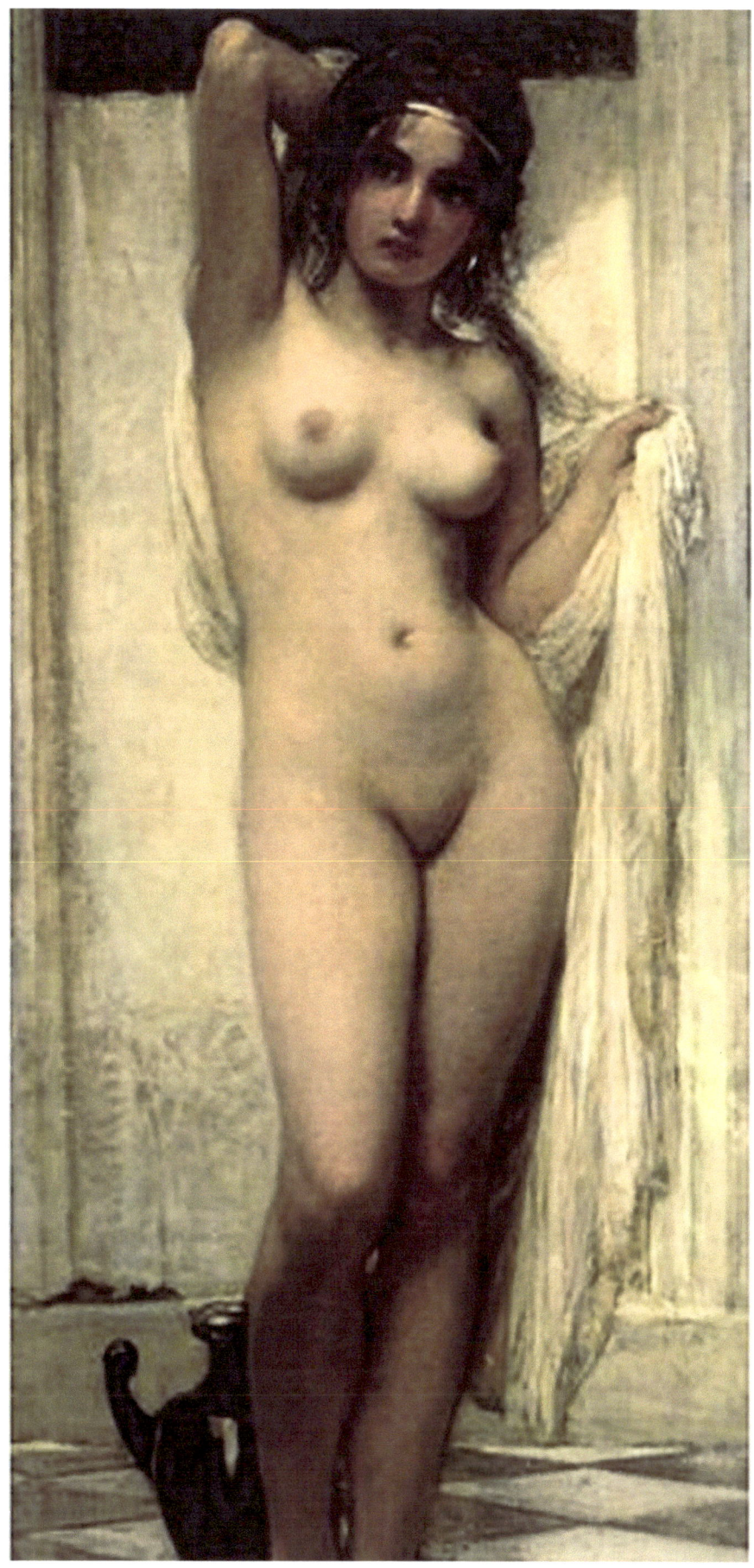

Artist & Year Unknown

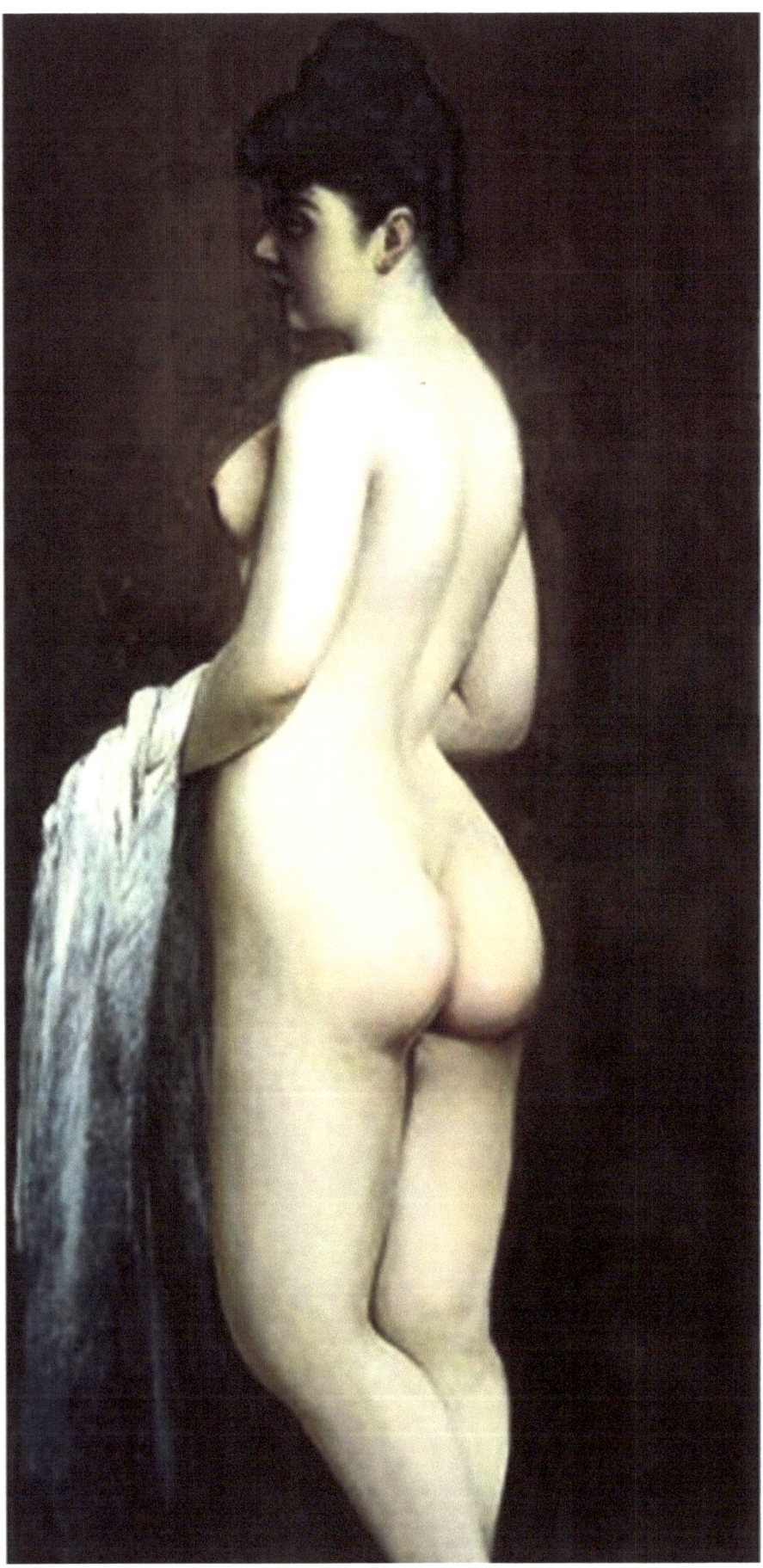

Artist & Year Unknown

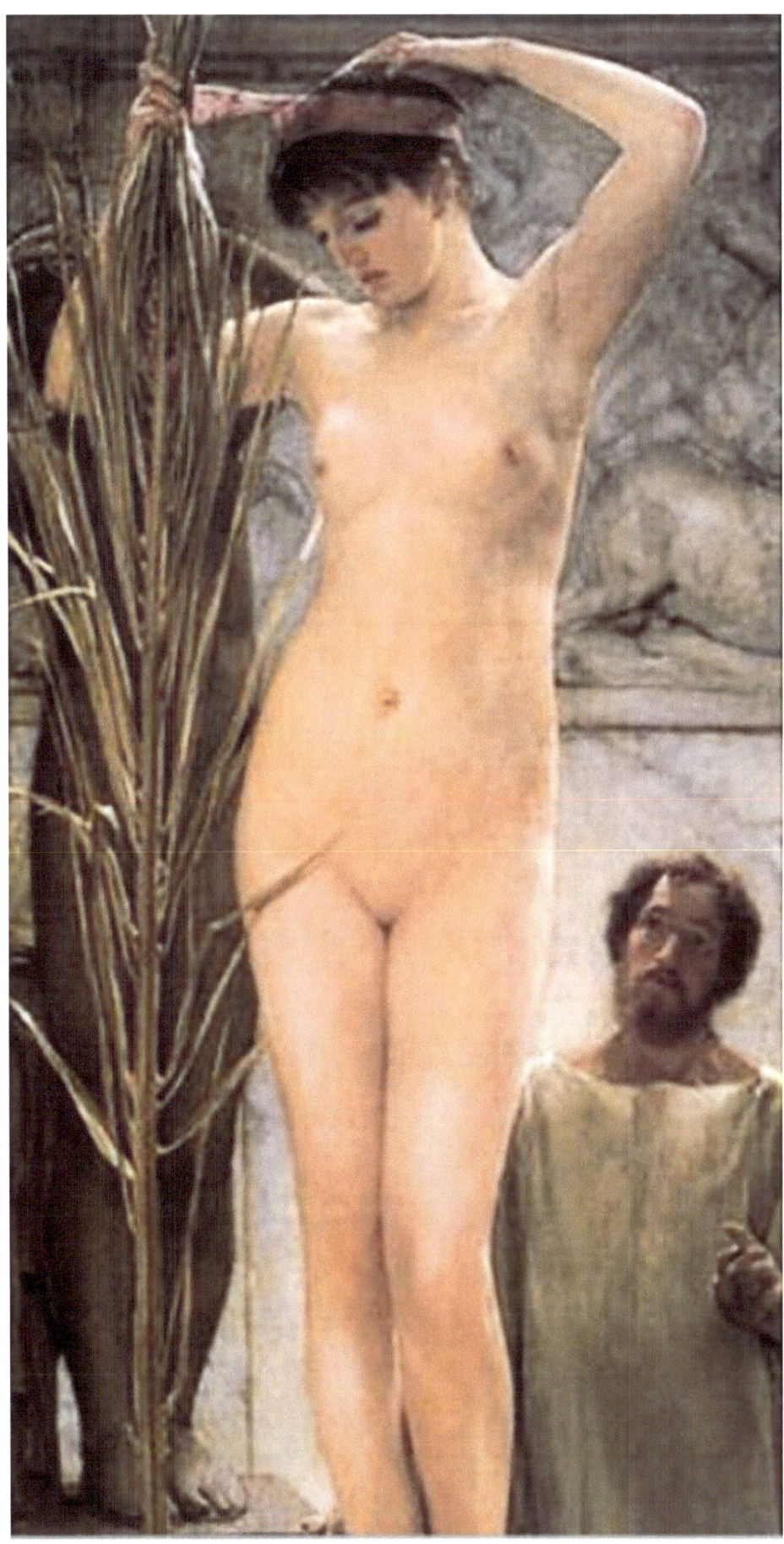

Artist & Year Unknown

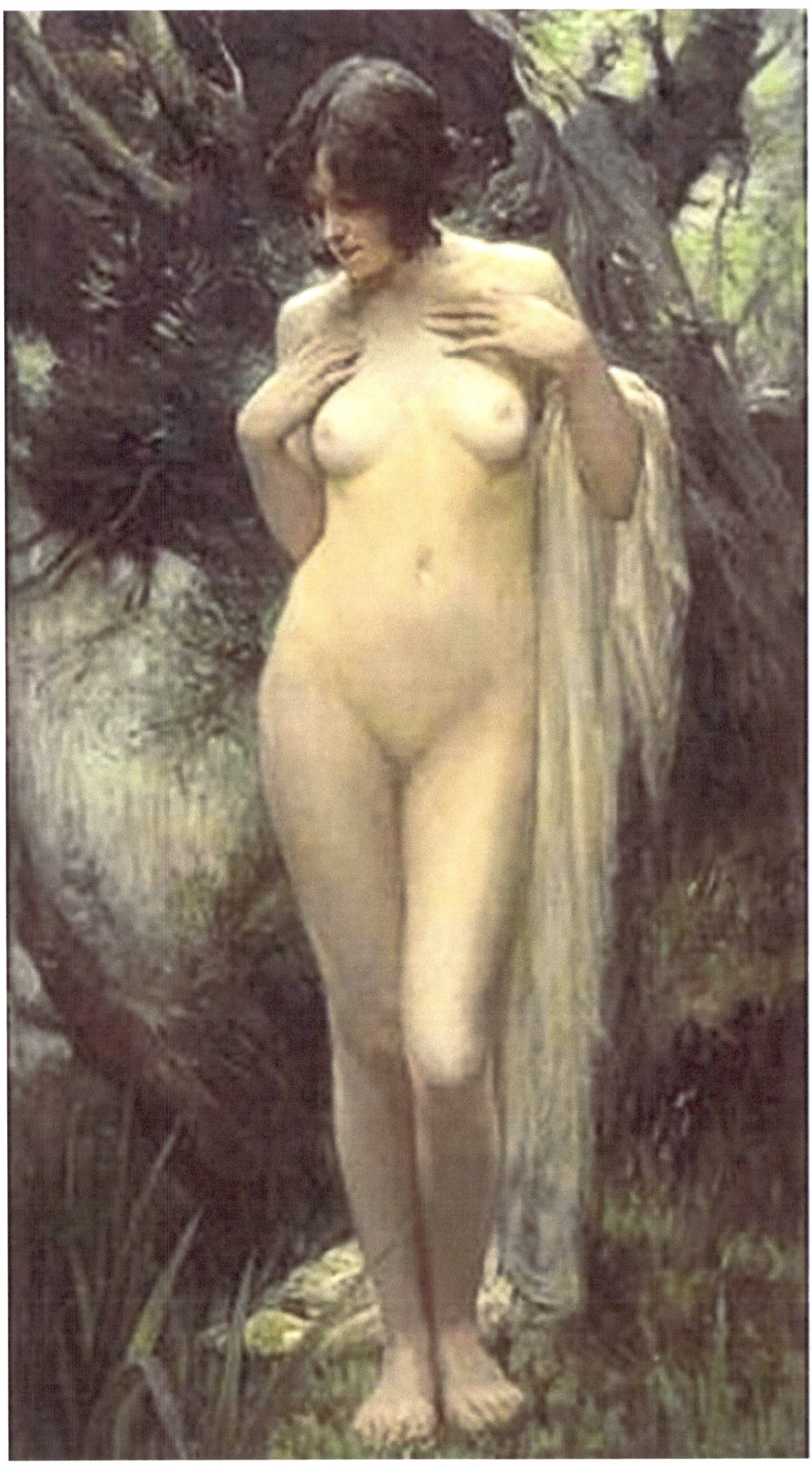

Artist & Year Unknown

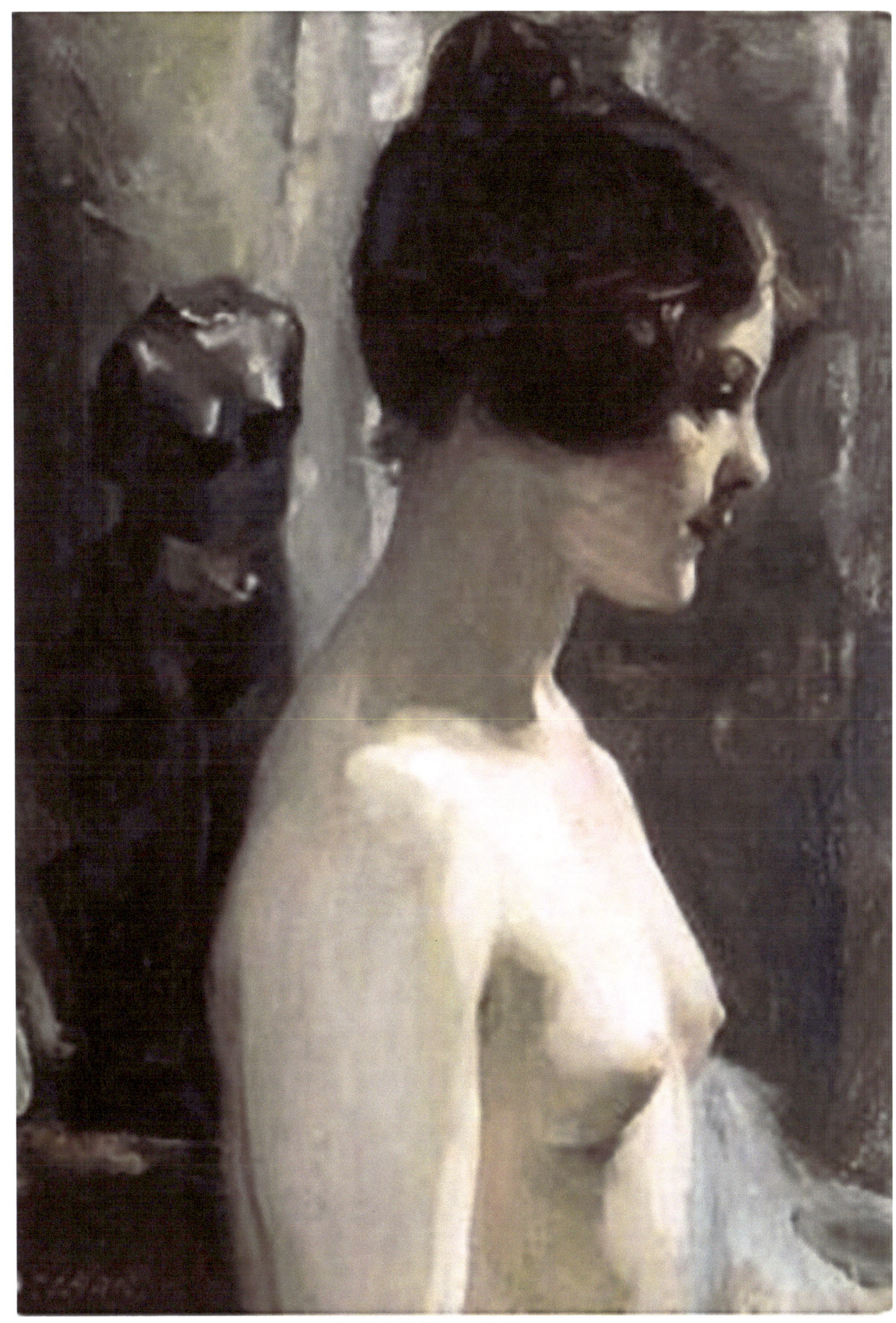

Artist & Year Unknown

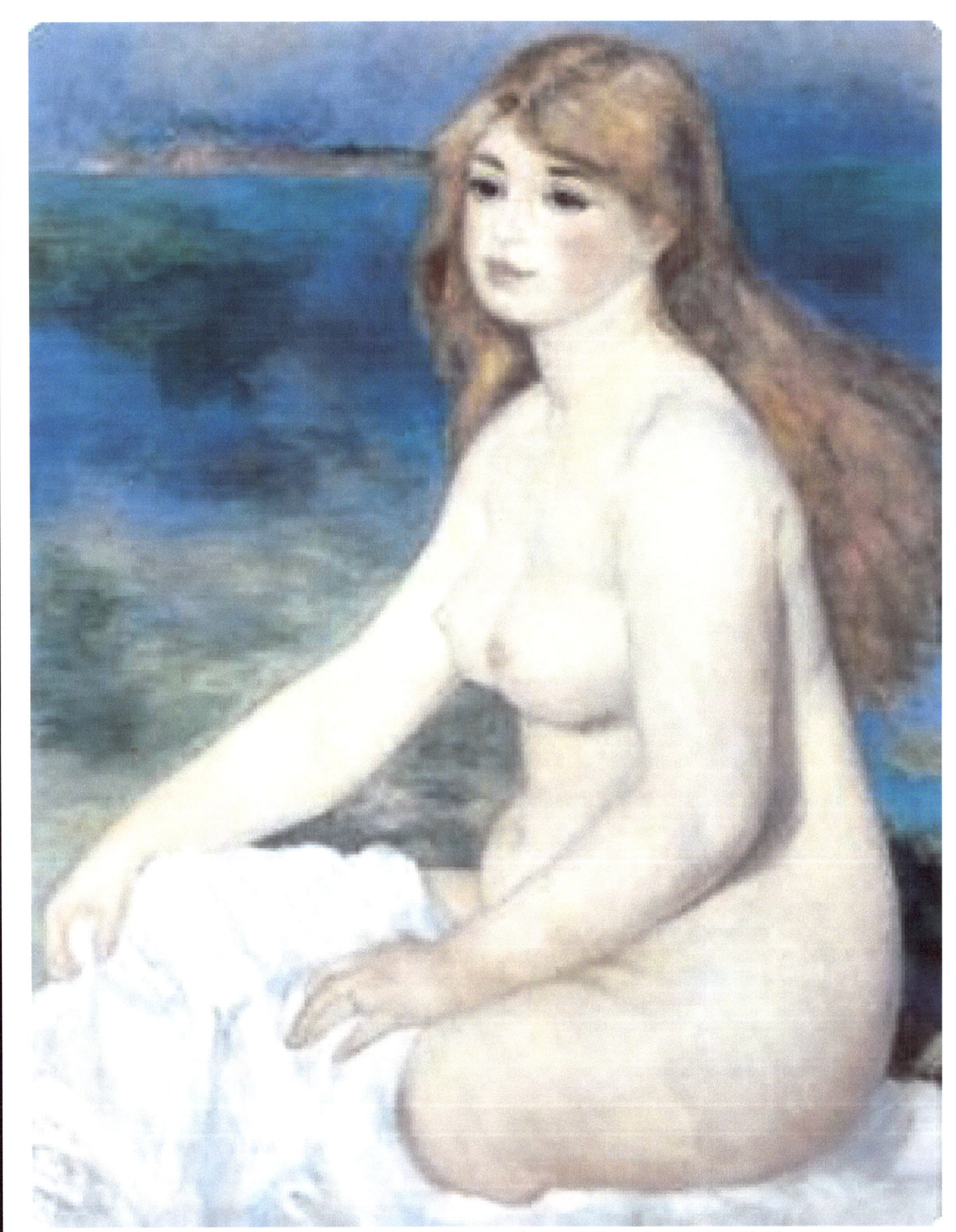

La Baigneuse Blond – by Pierre-August Renoir, 1841-1919

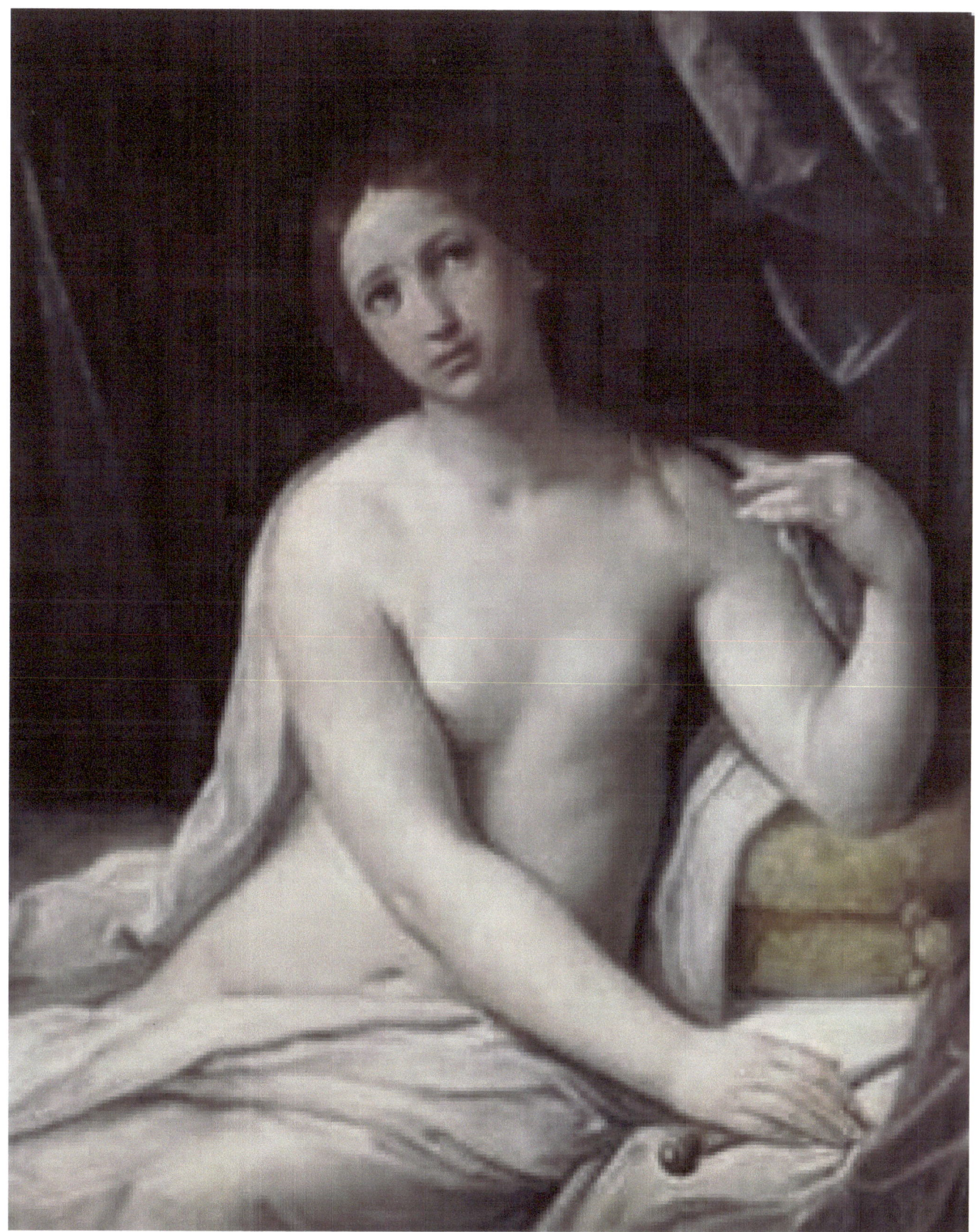

Lucrezia Romana – Artist & Year Unknown

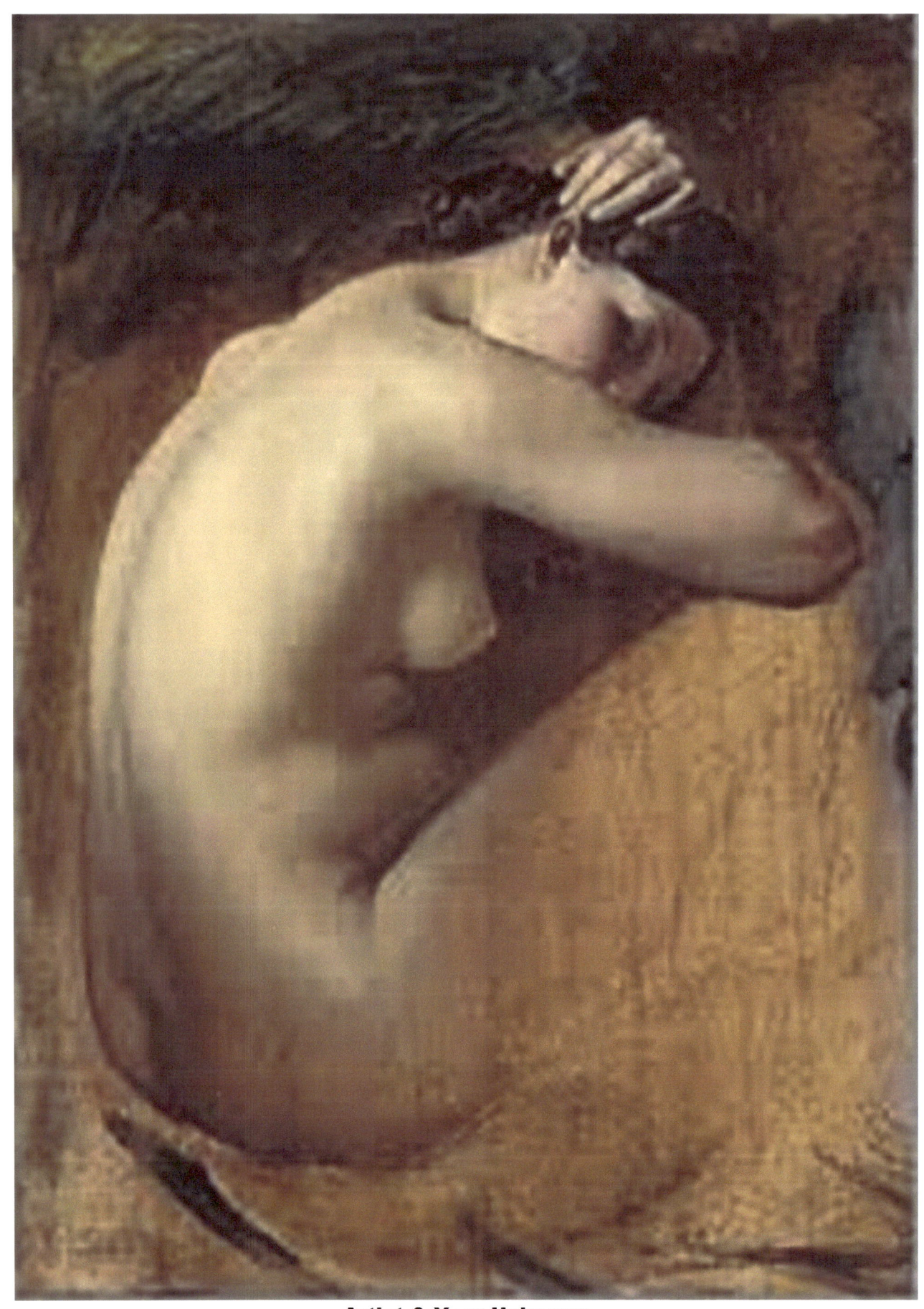

Artist & Year Unknown

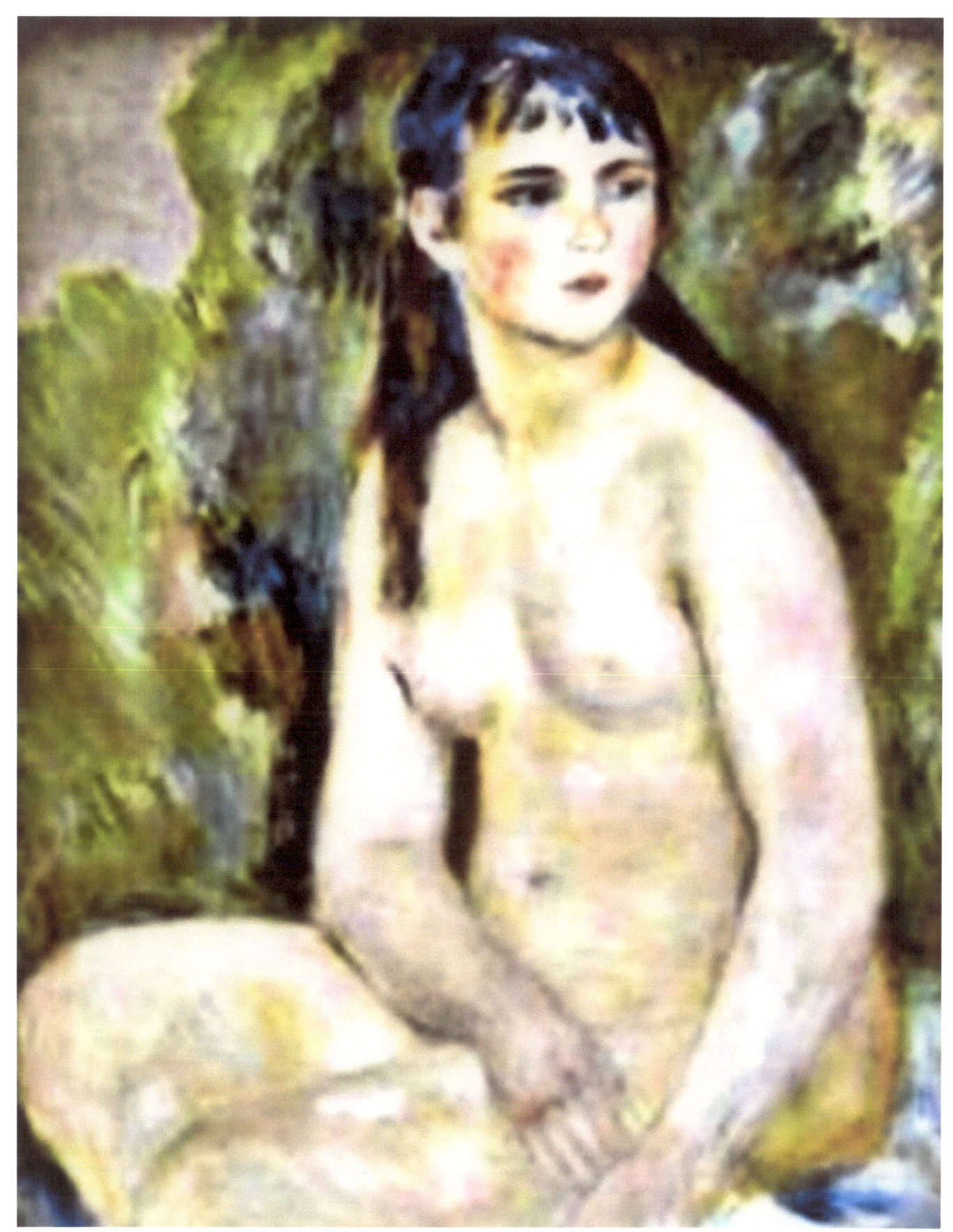

Artist & Year Unknown

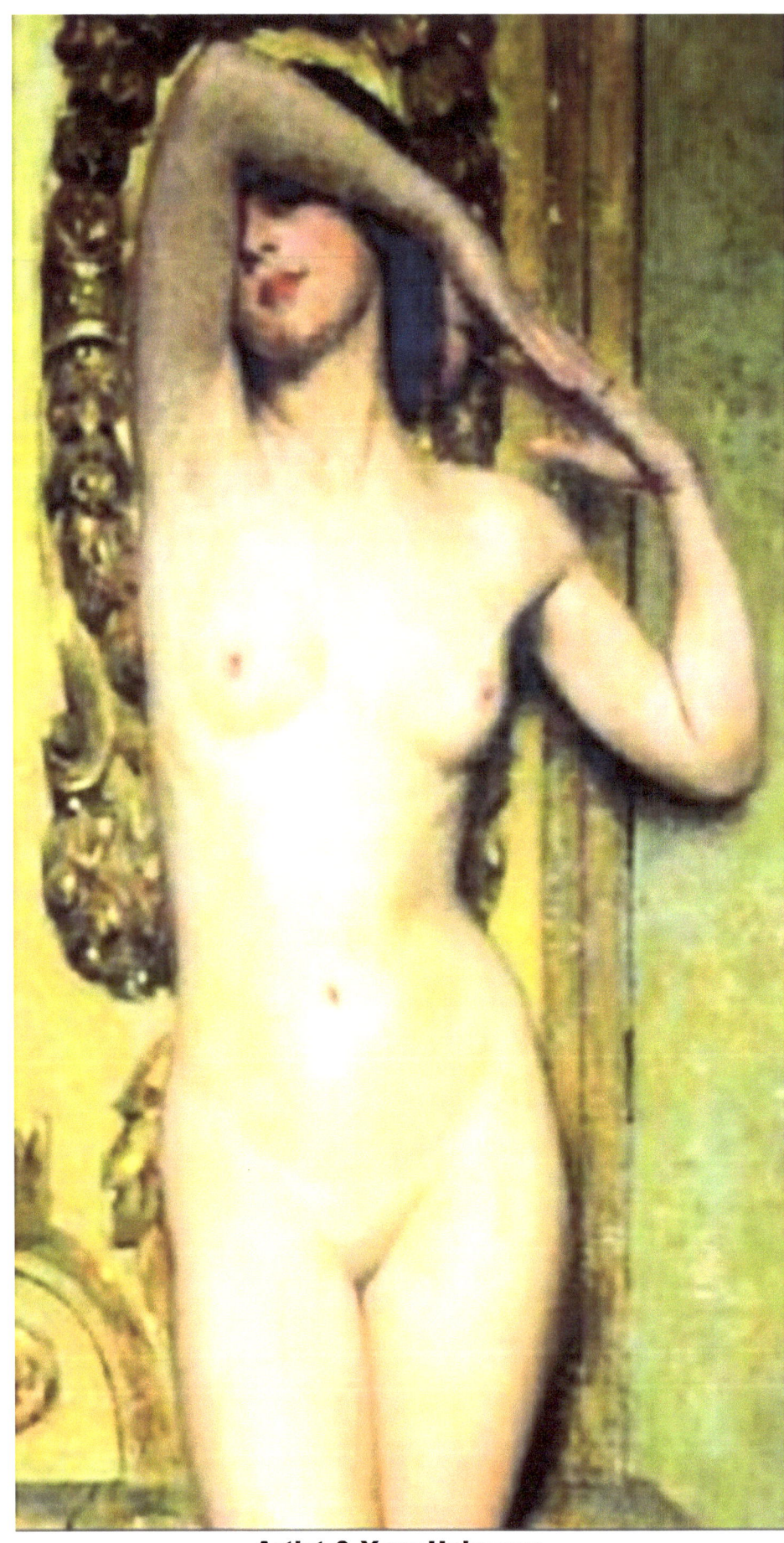

Artist & Year Unknown

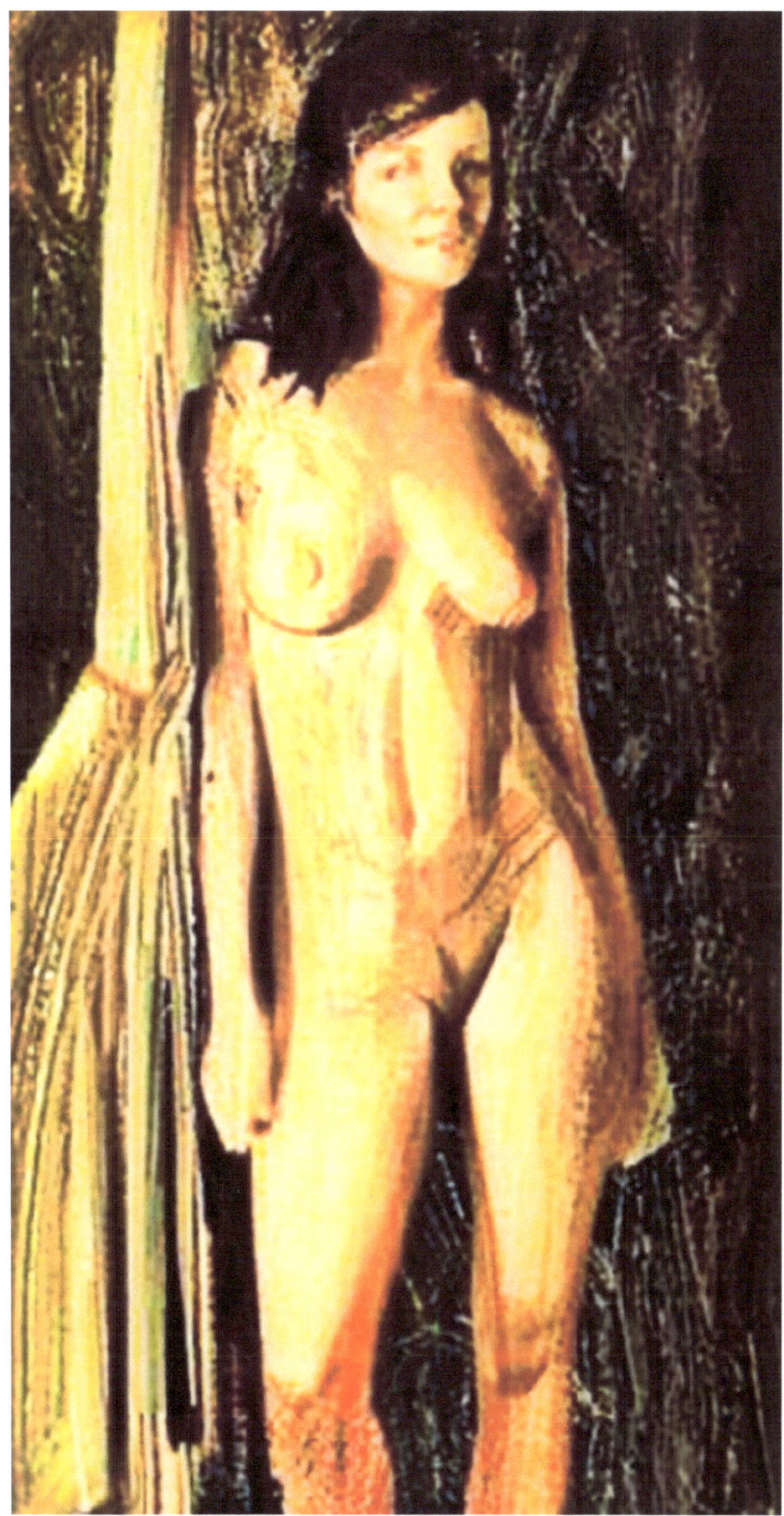

Artist & Year Unknown

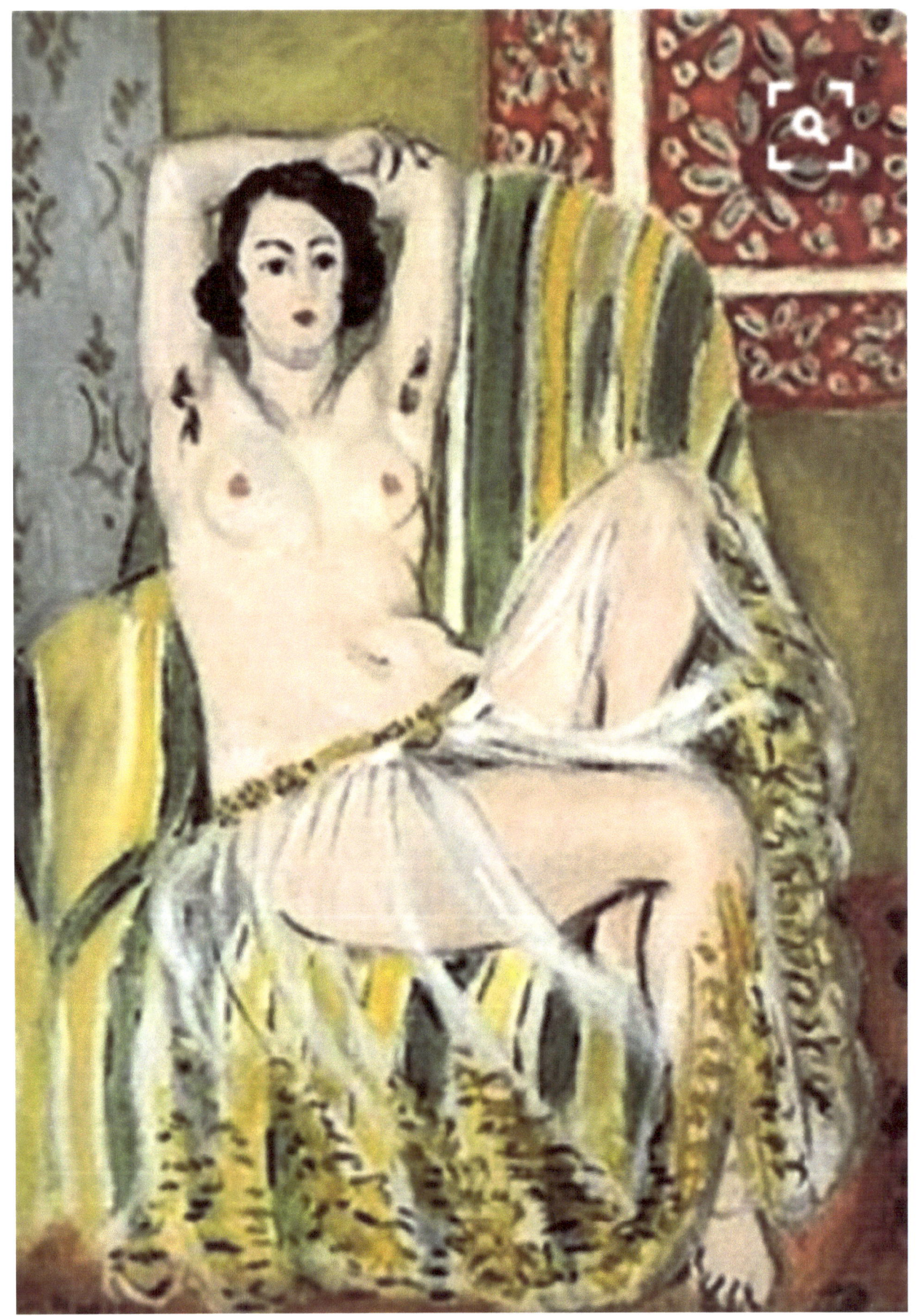

Artist & Year Unknown

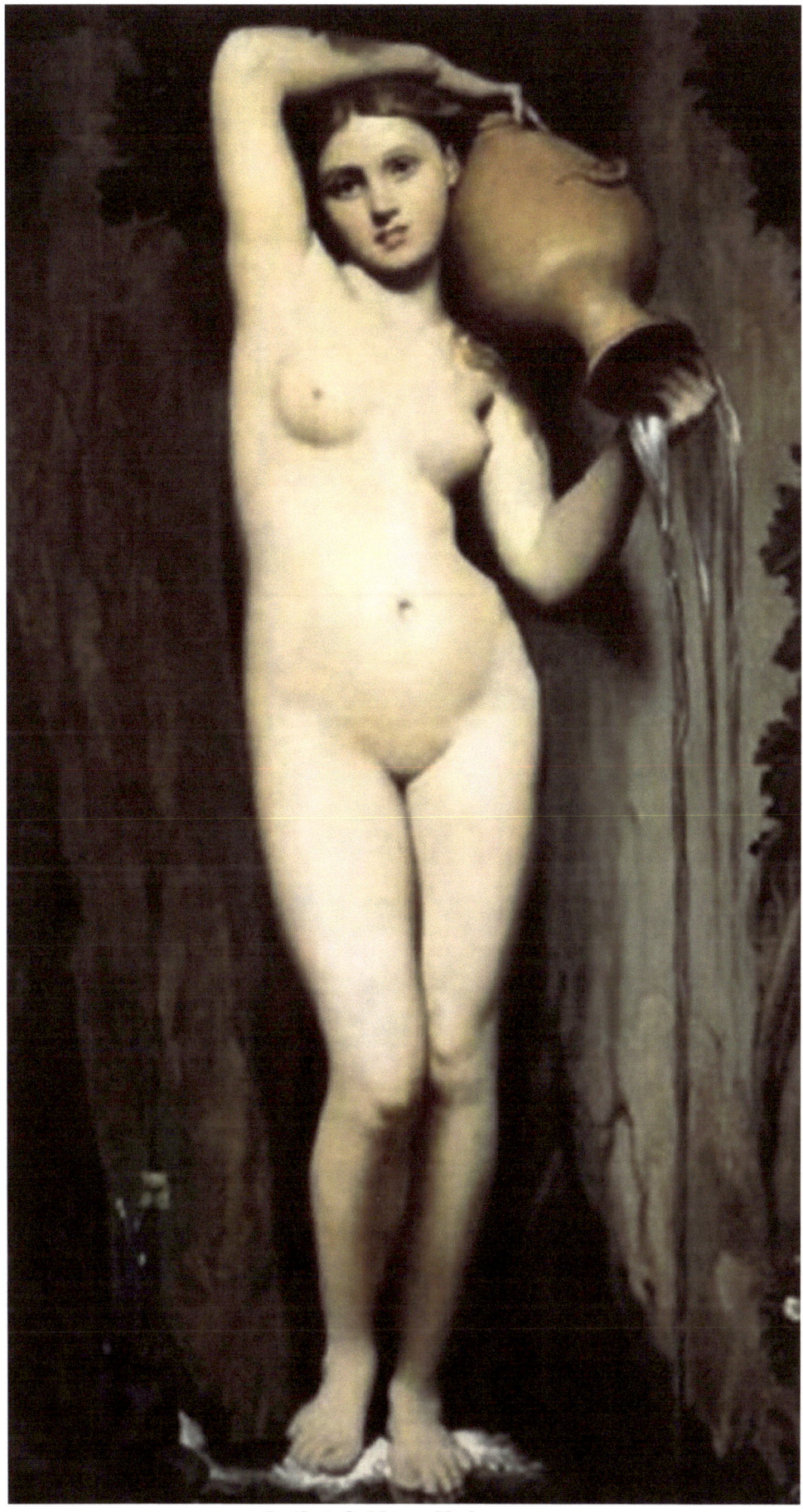

Artist & Year Unknown

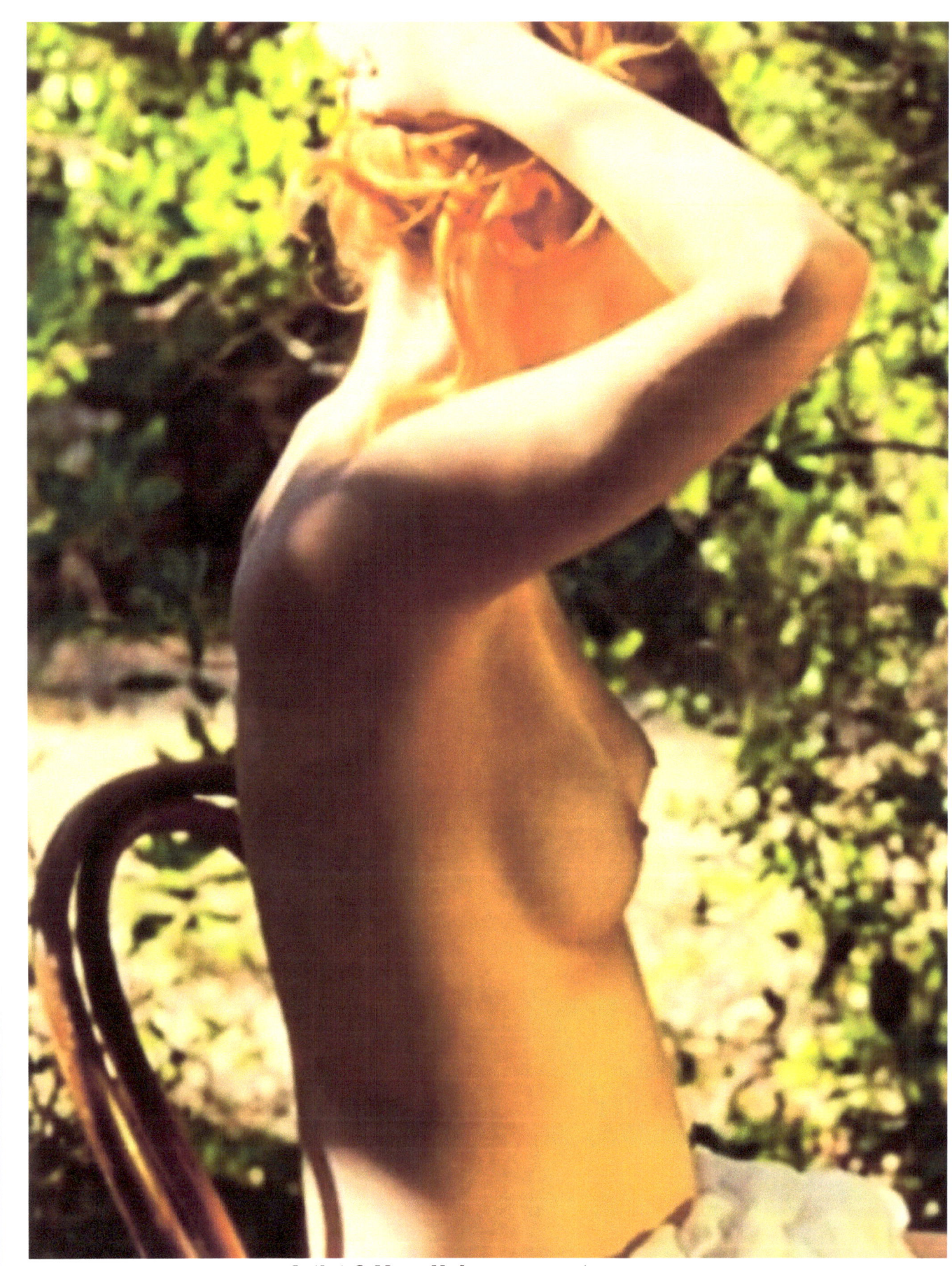

Artist & Year Unknown, contemporary

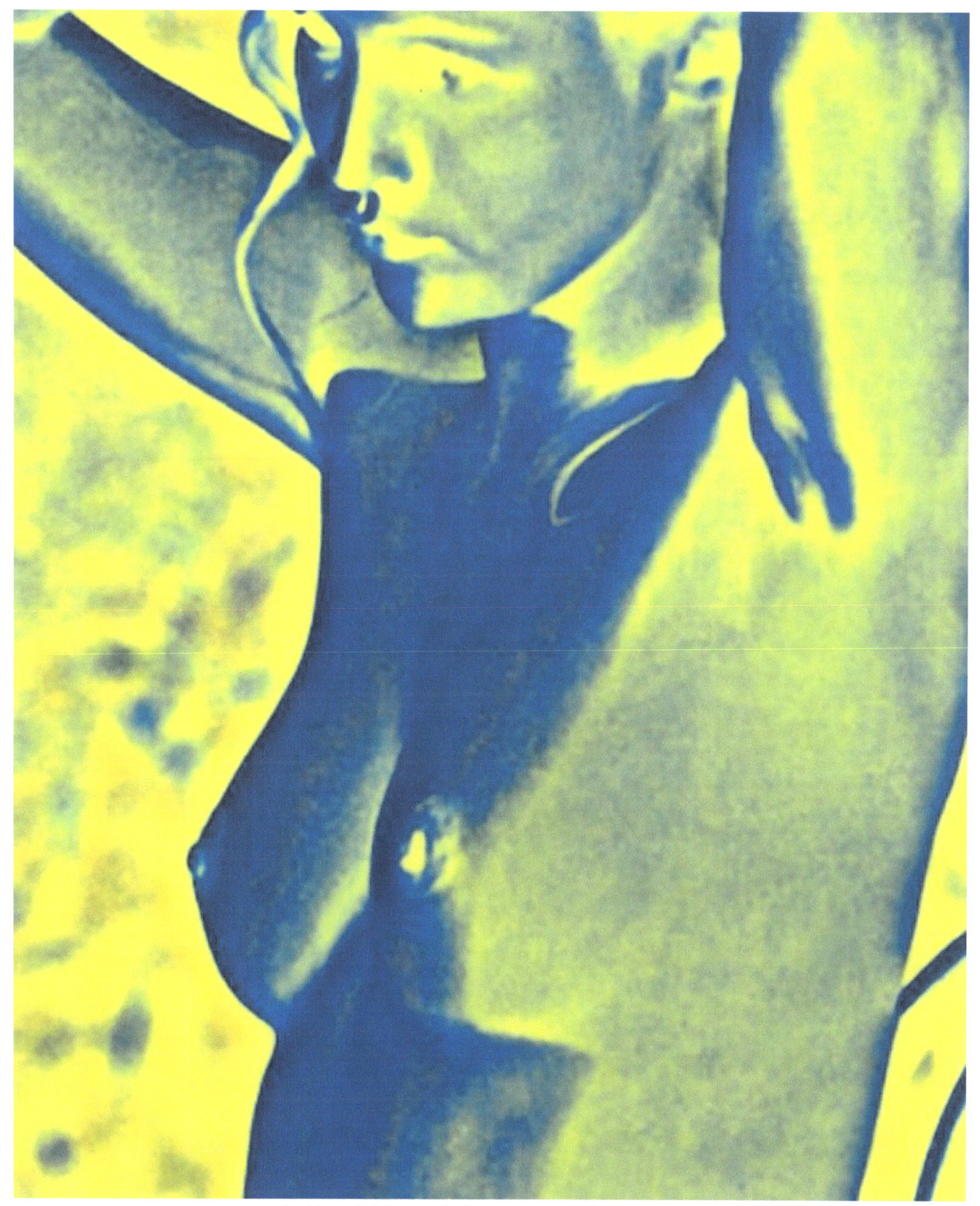

Artist & Year Unknown, contemporary

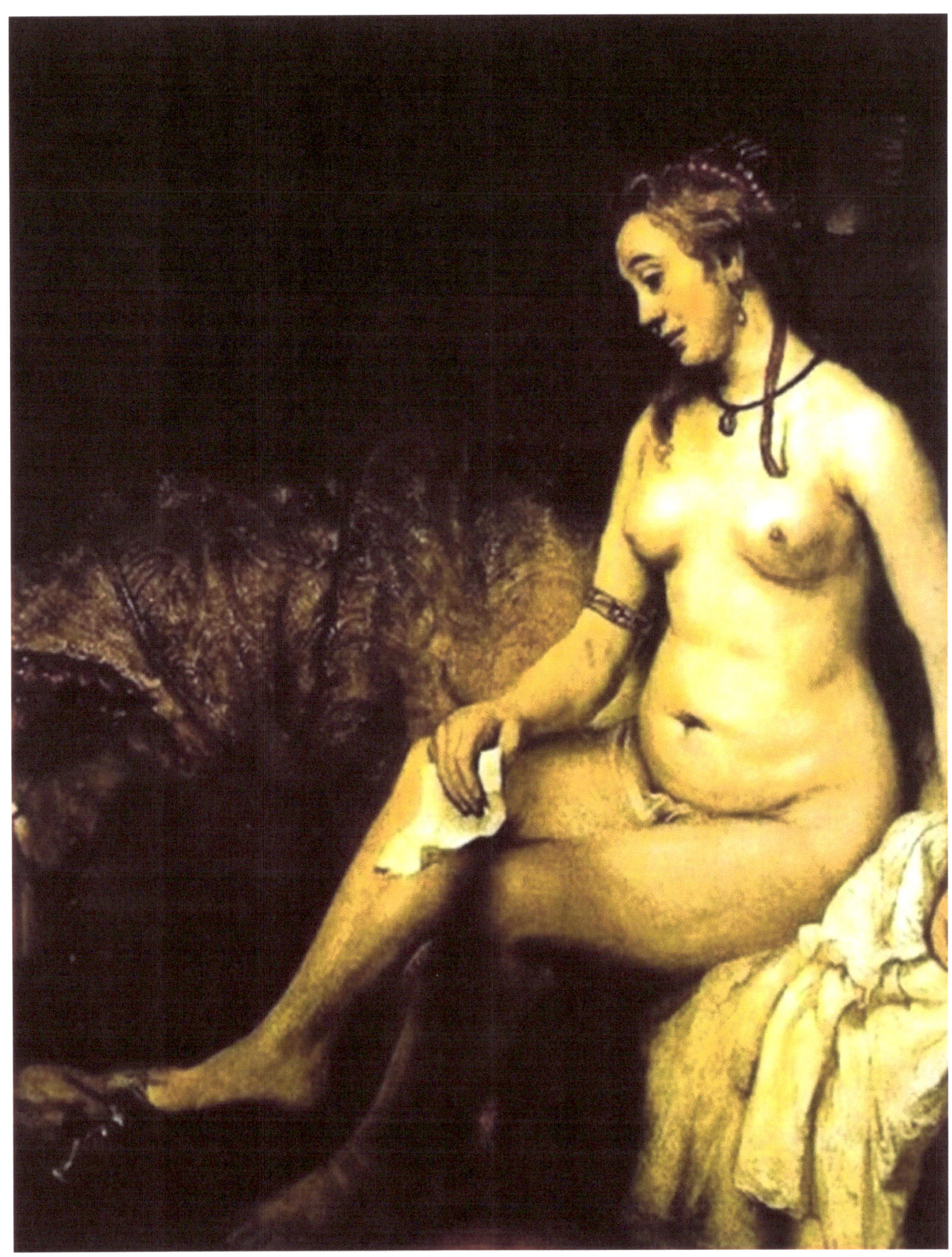

Artist & Year Unknown

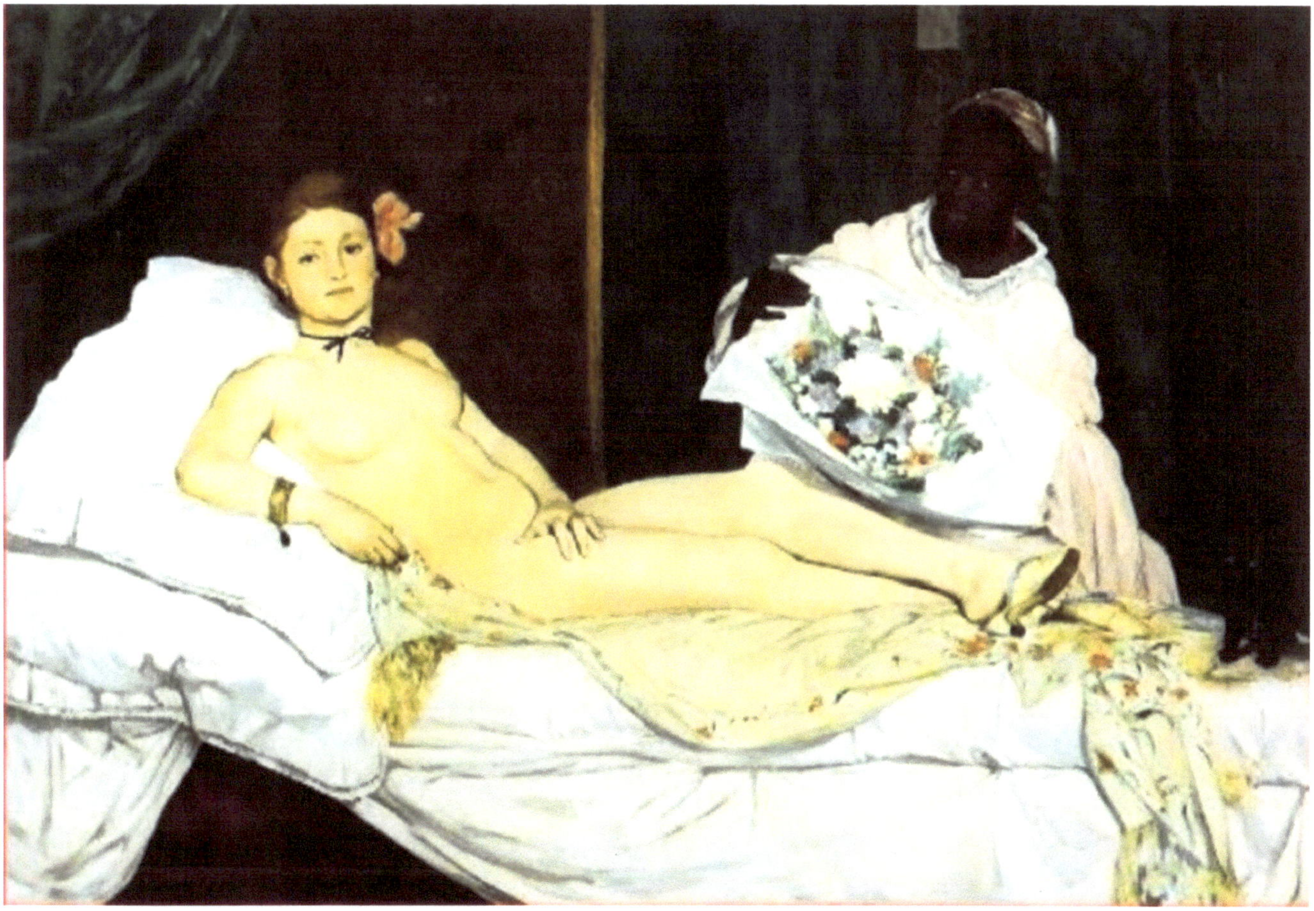

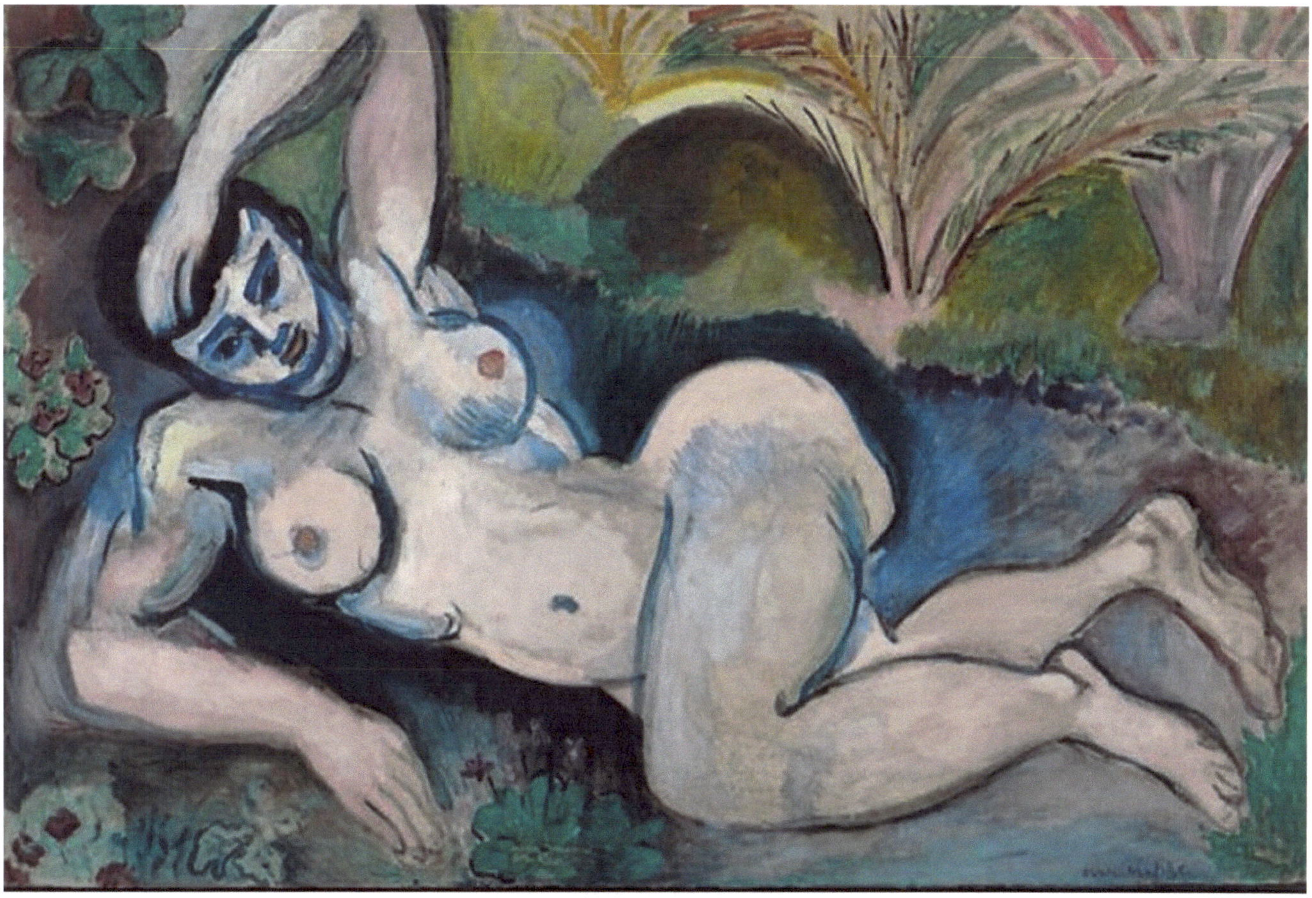

Artists & Years Unknown

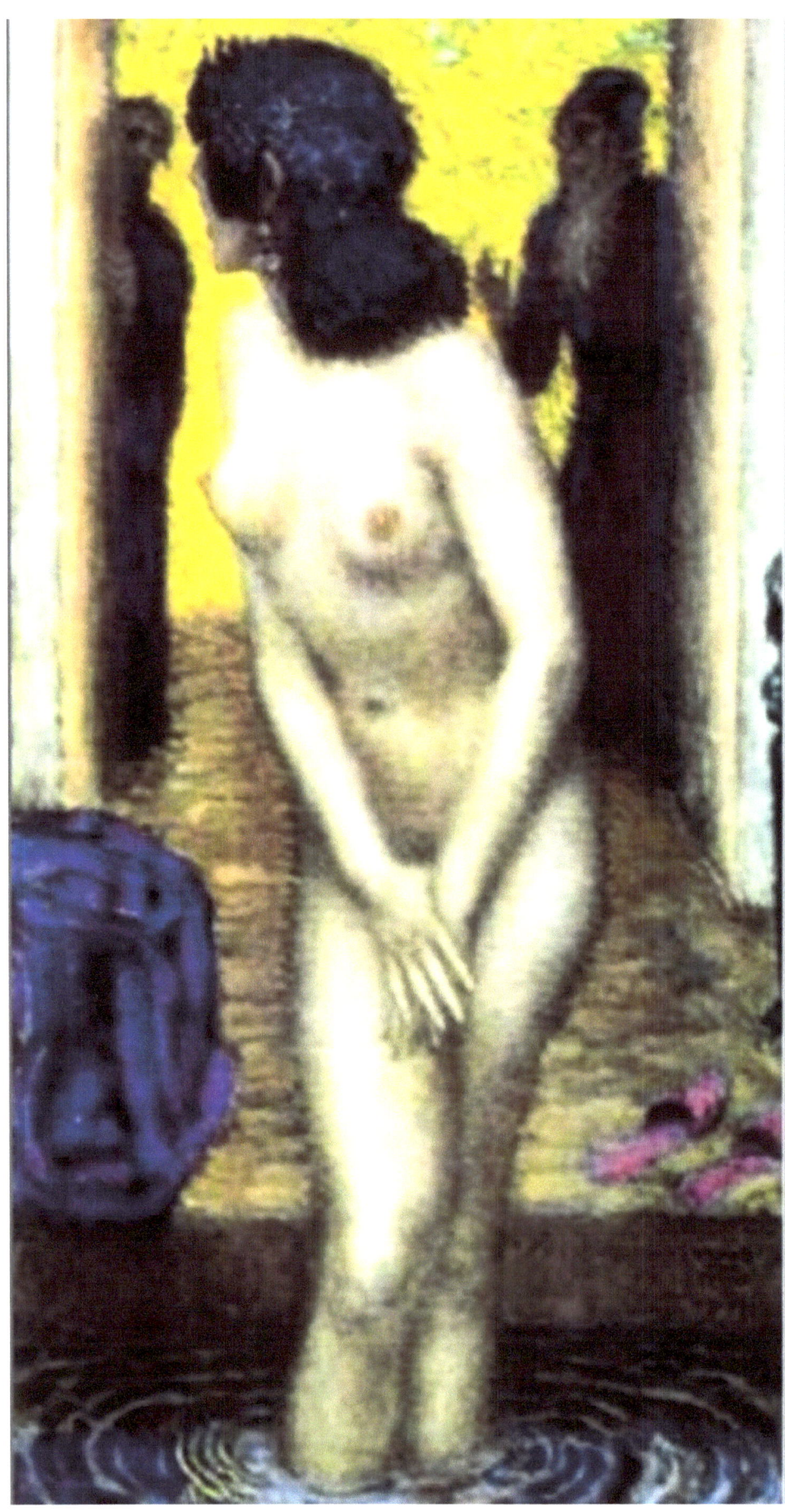

Artist & Year Unknown

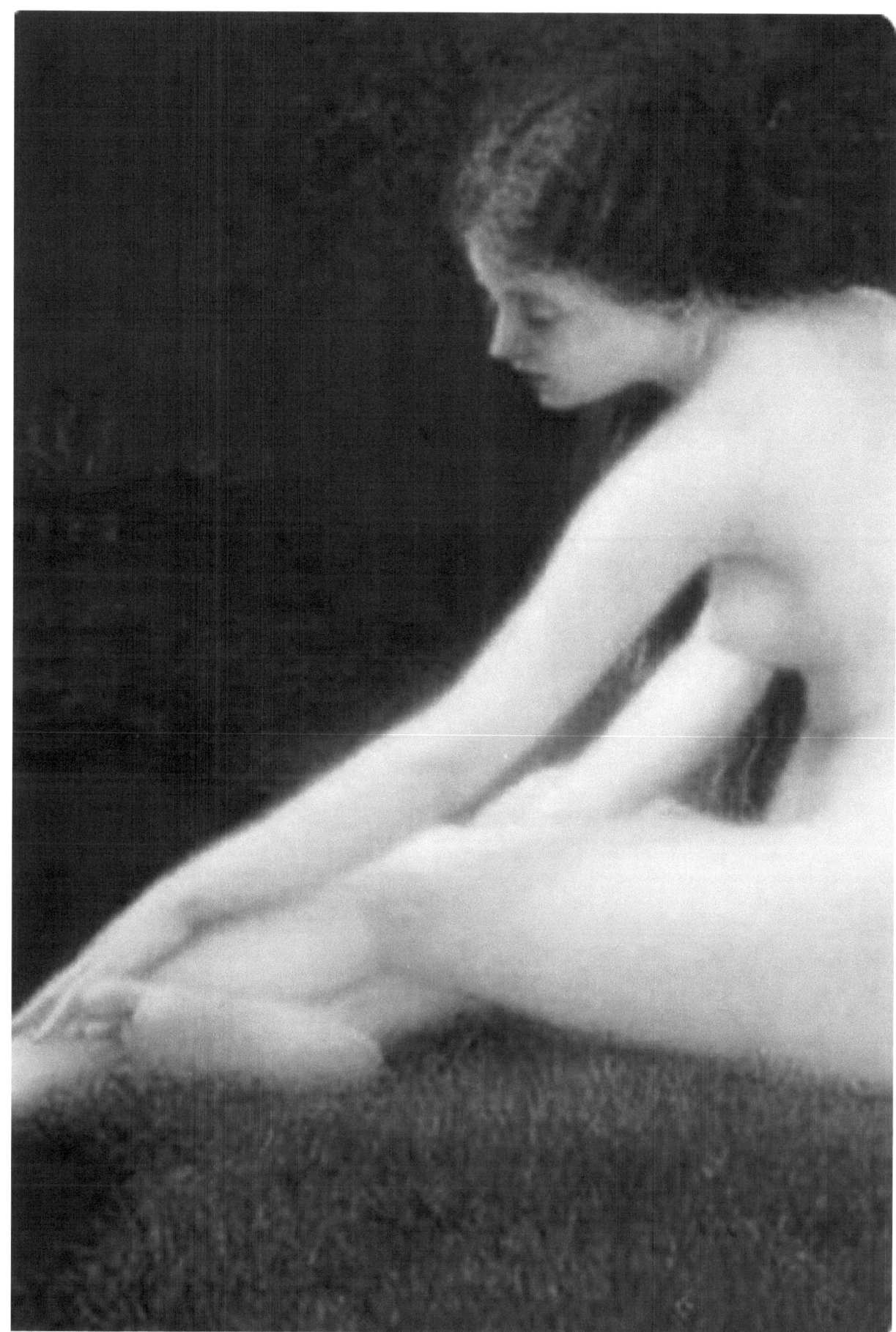

Nymph, by William Jacob Baer, 1898

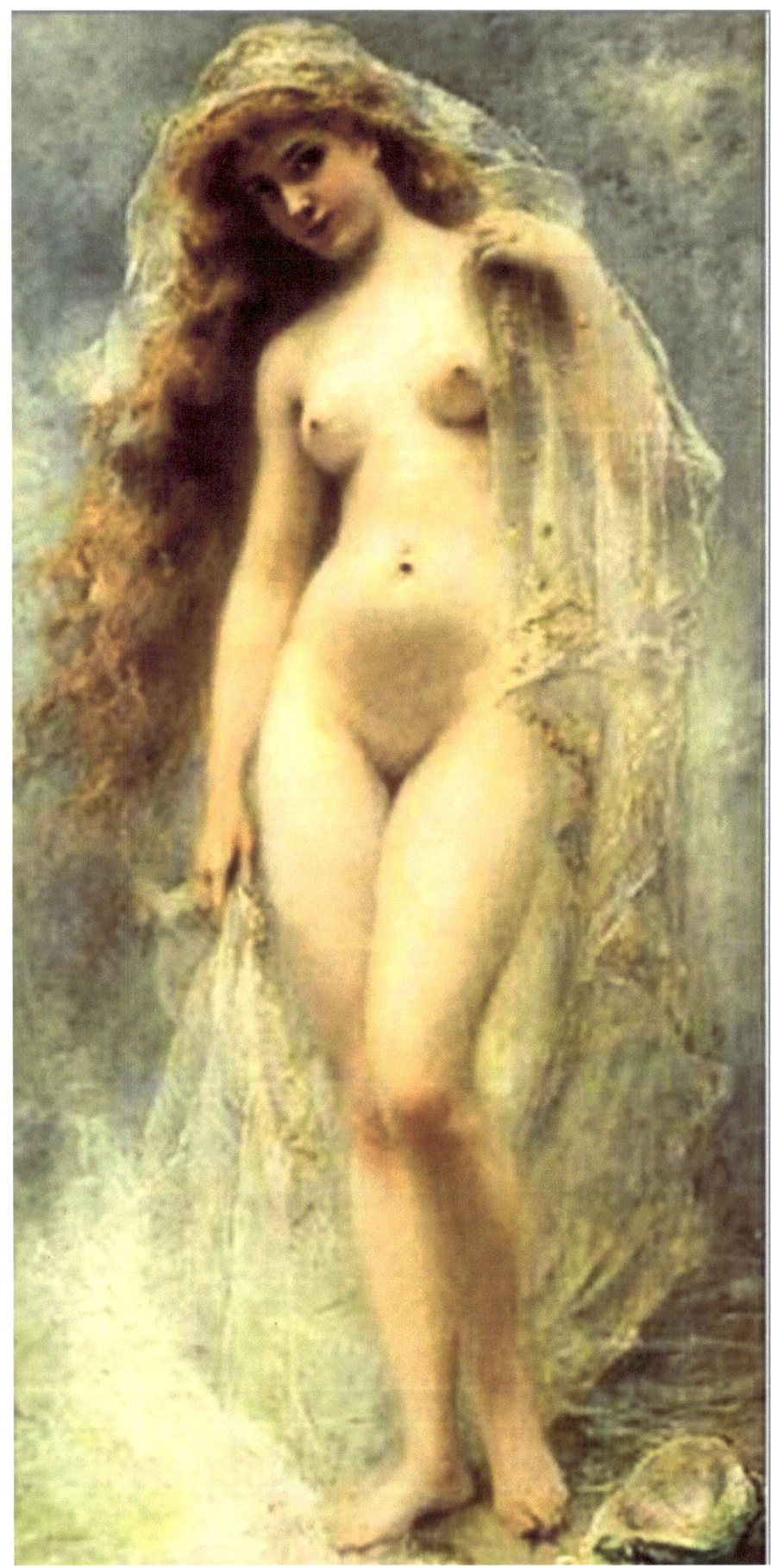

Birth of Venus, by Konstantin MaKovsky, 1839 – 1915

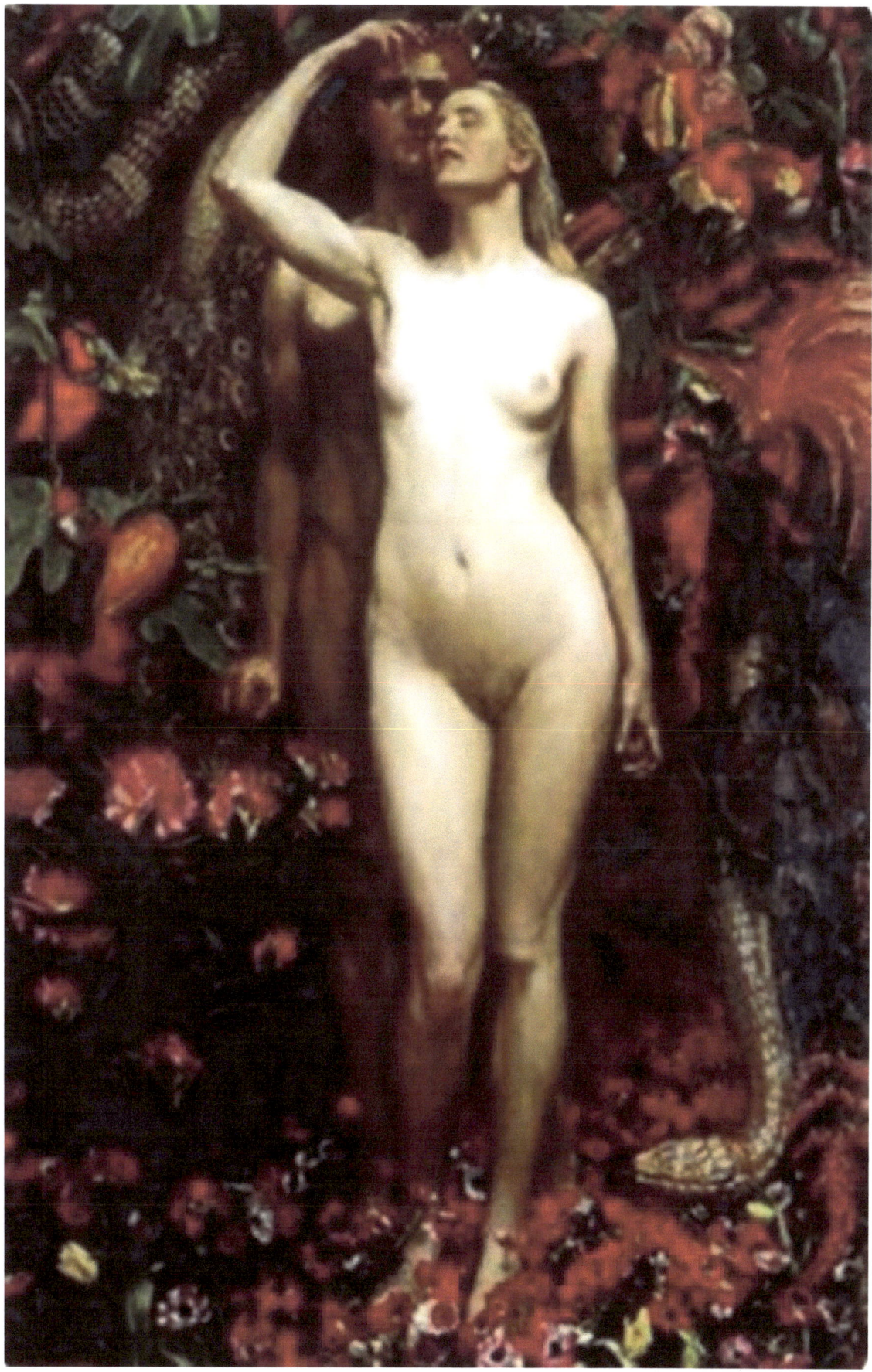

The Woman, the Man and the Serpent – By John Bryant Liston, 1911

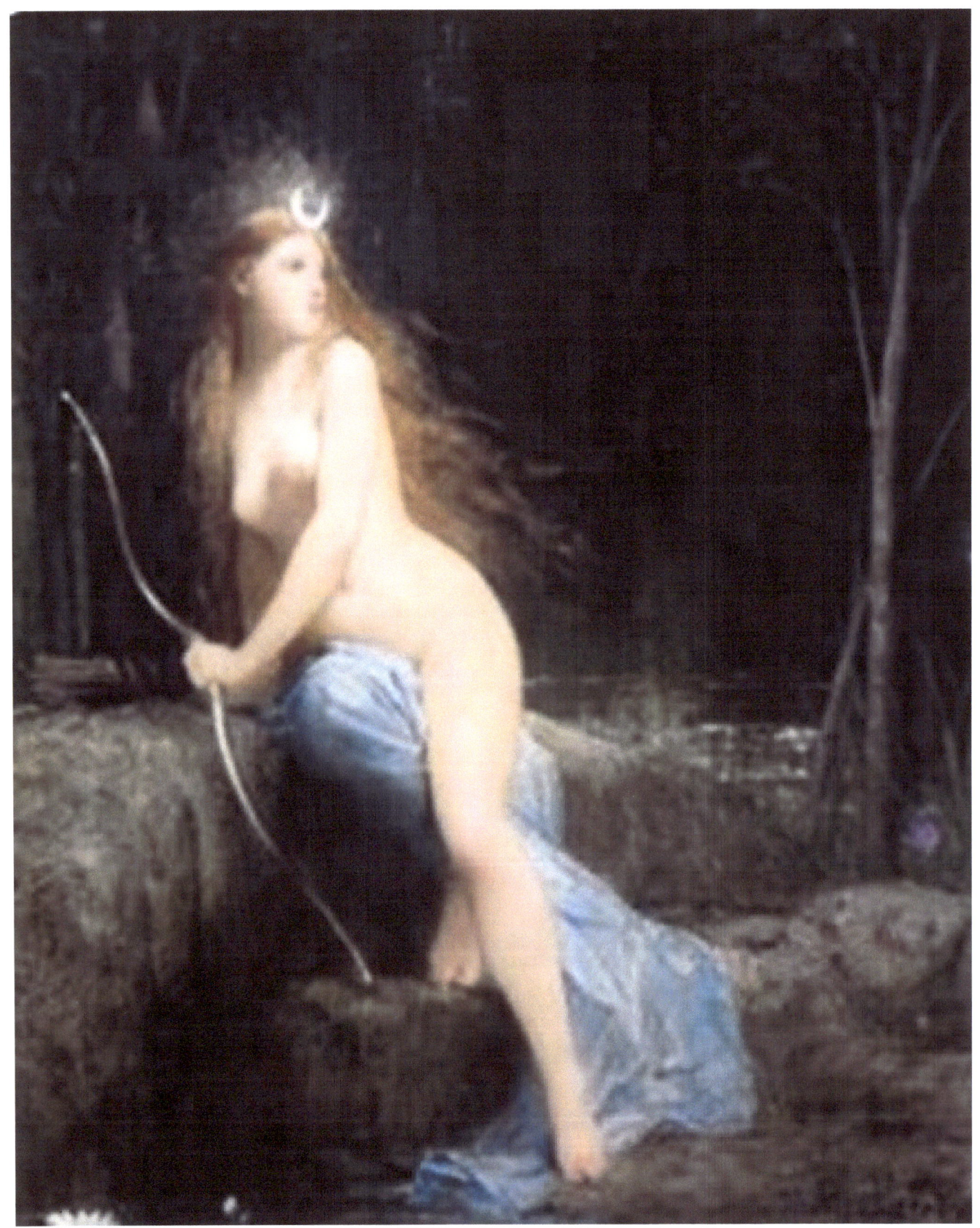

Diana, 1879, by Jules Joseph Lefebre

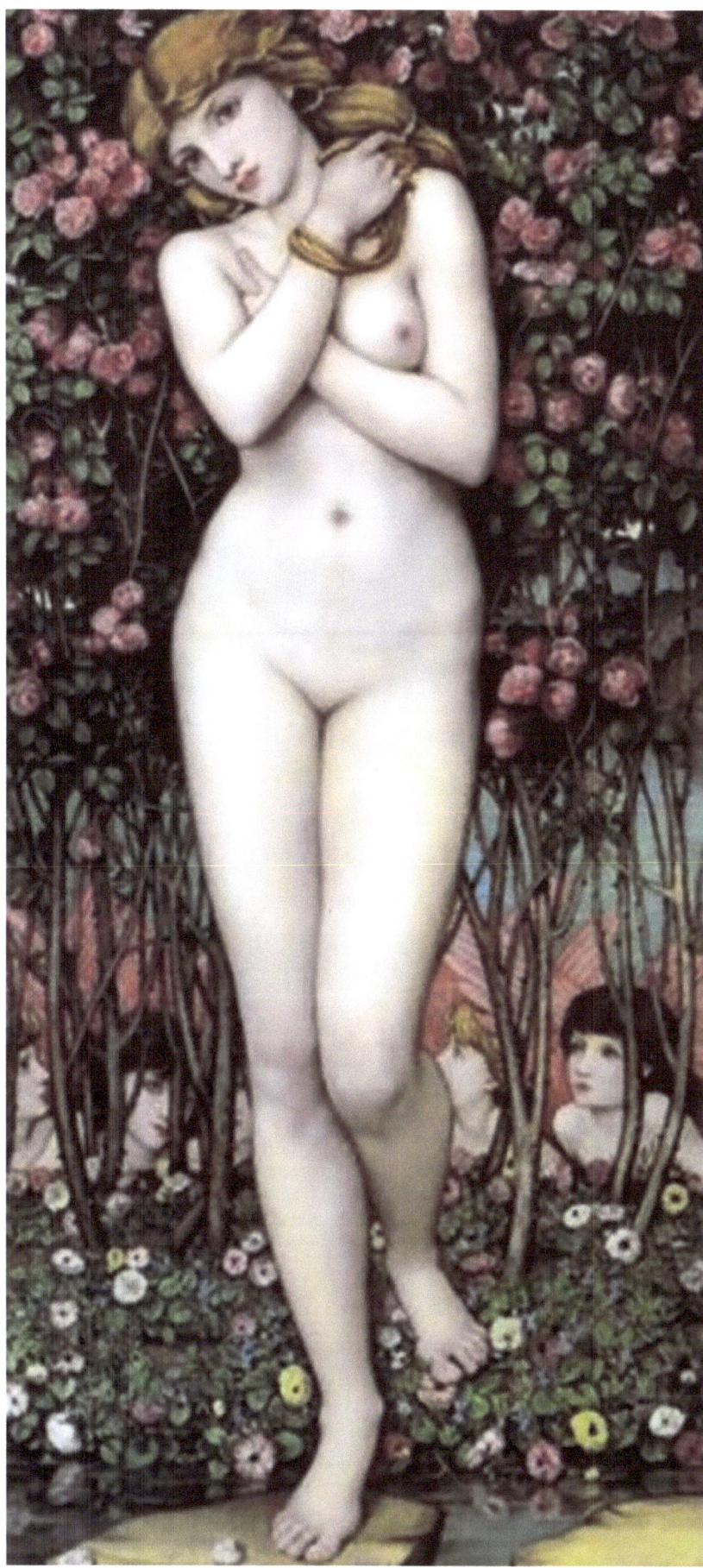

Flora – by John Roddam Spencer Stanhope, 1889

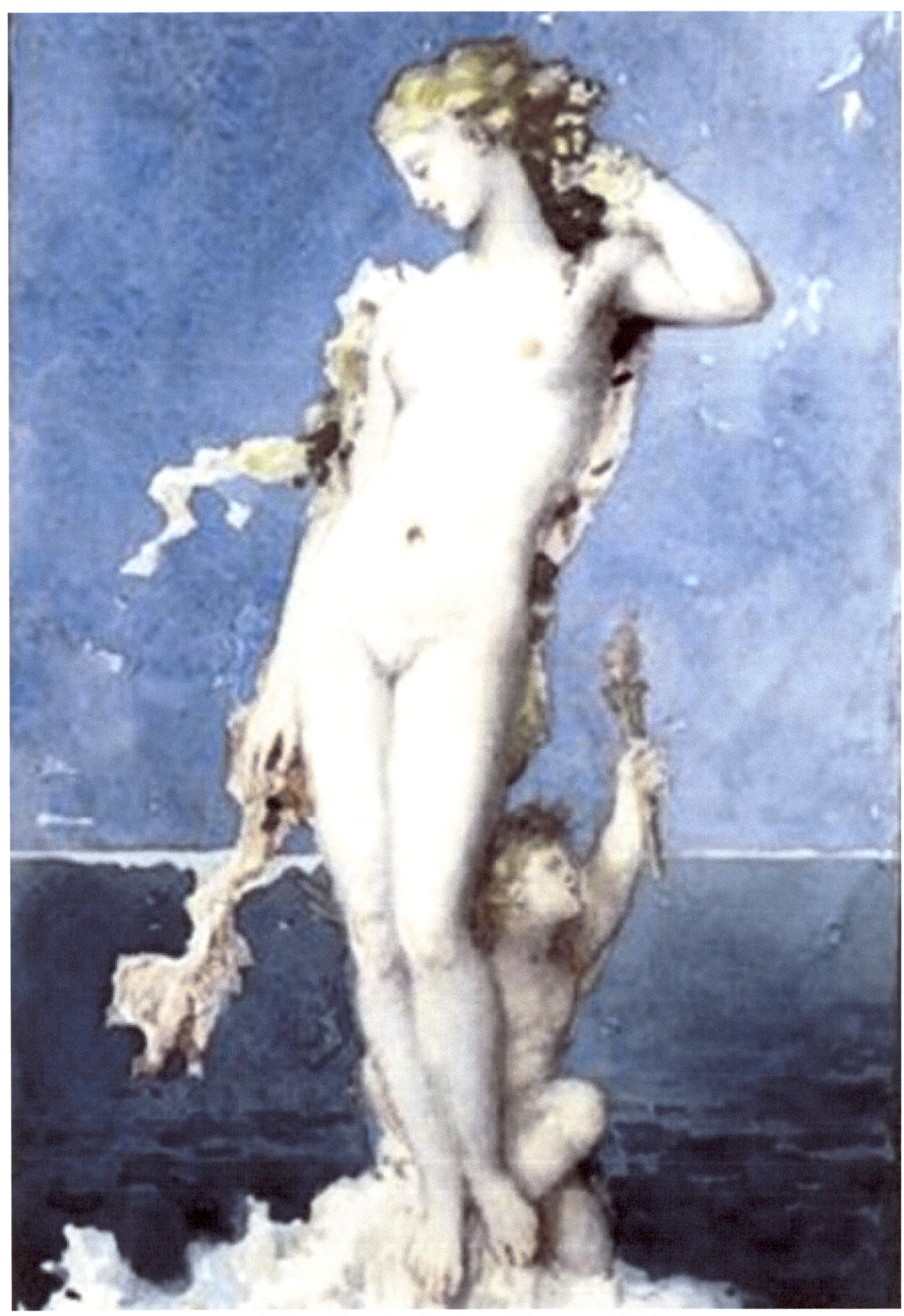

Aphrodite – by Gustave Moreau, 1871

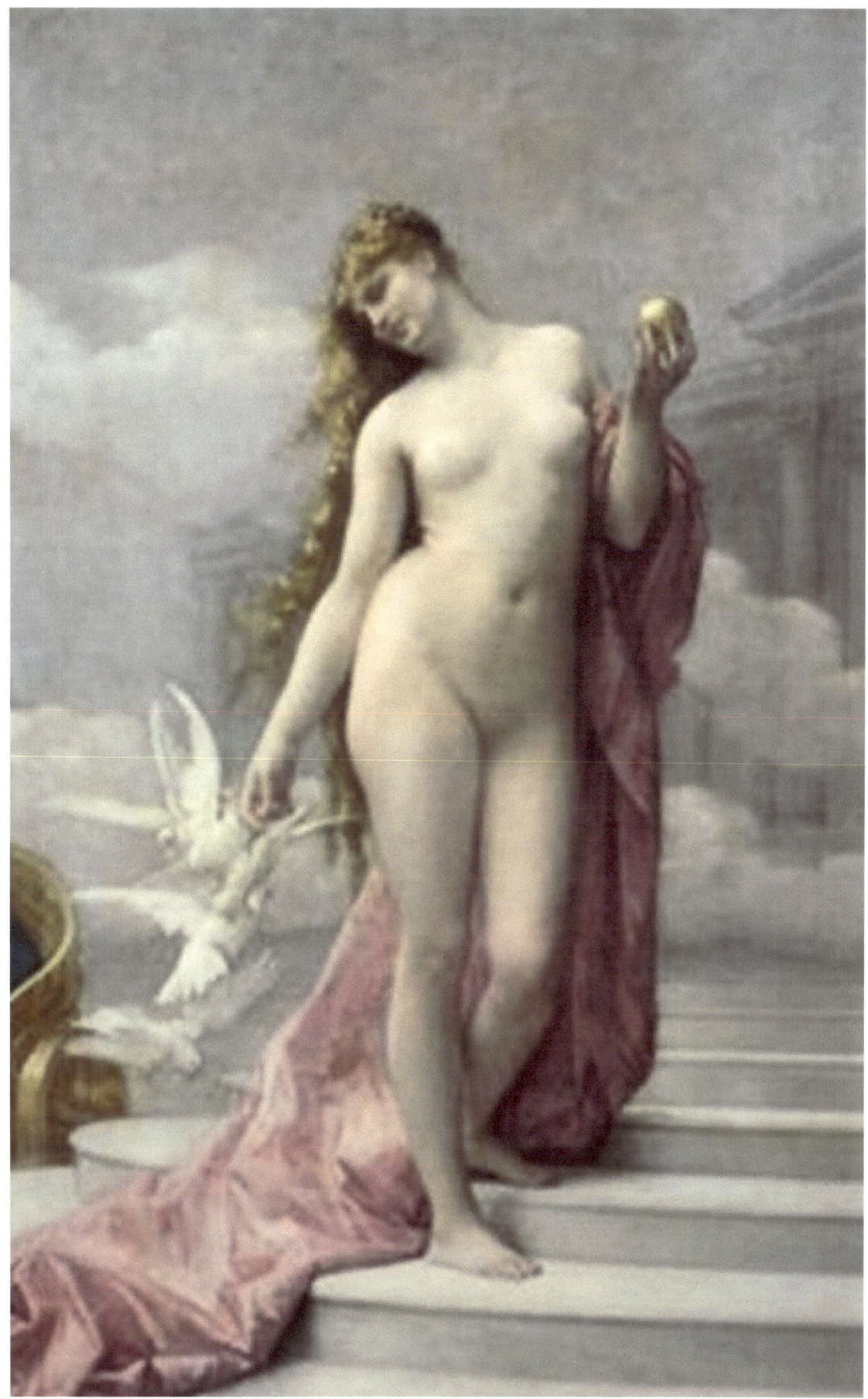

Venus – by Alexandre Cabanel, 1875

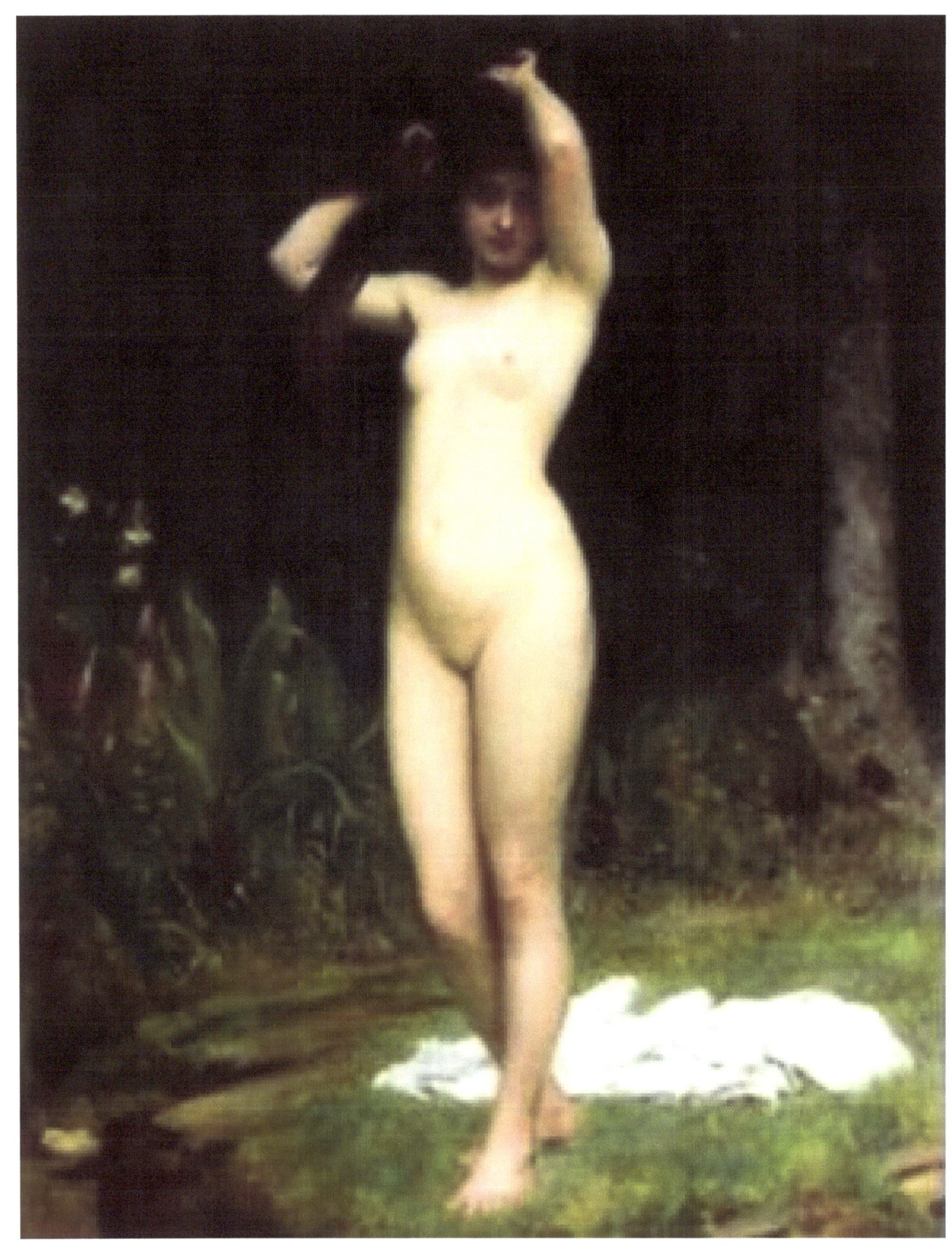

Vieni al mio lago – by Philip Hermogenes Calderon, 1833-1898

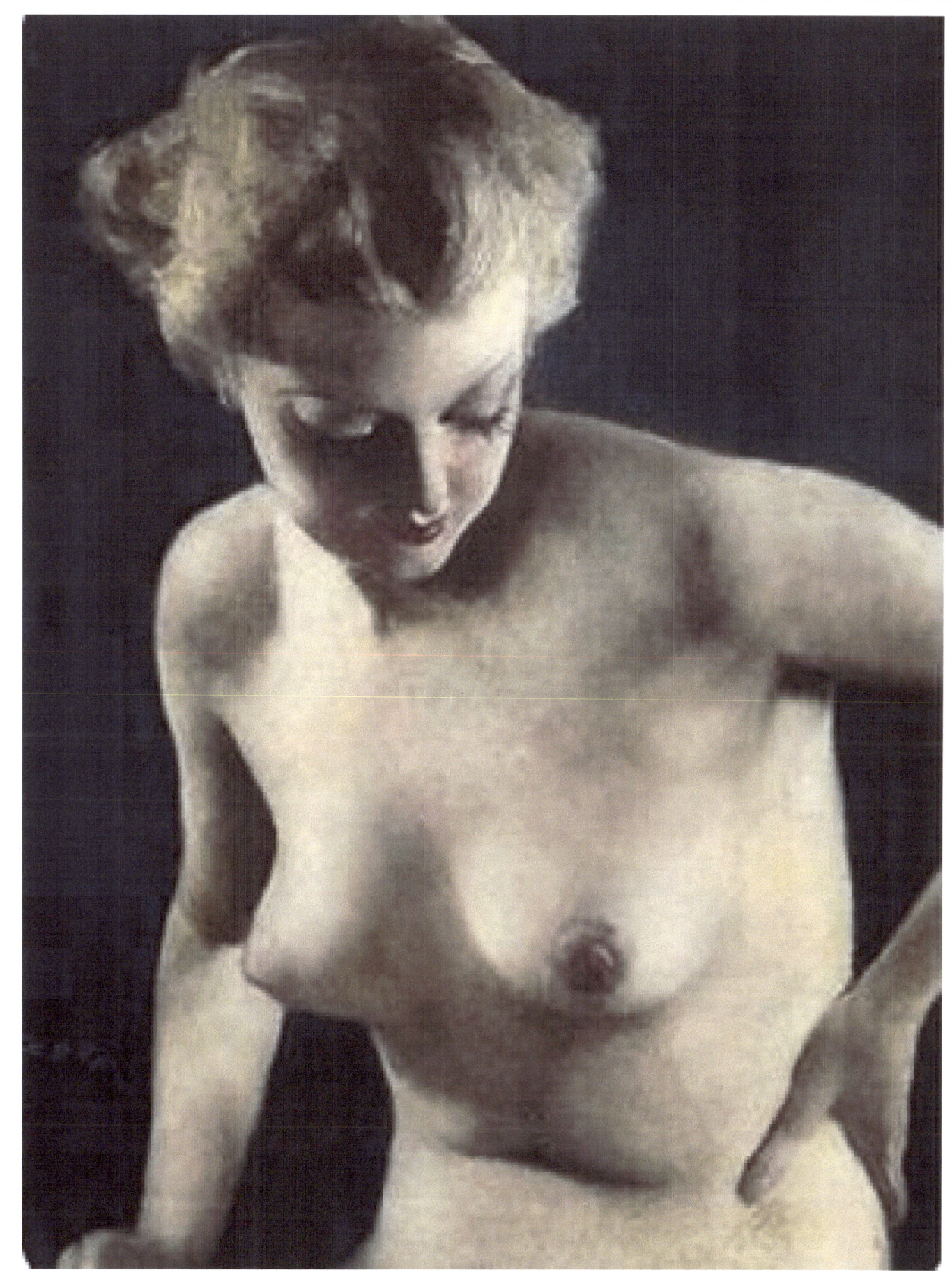

By Pal Friend, Hungary, 1893-1976

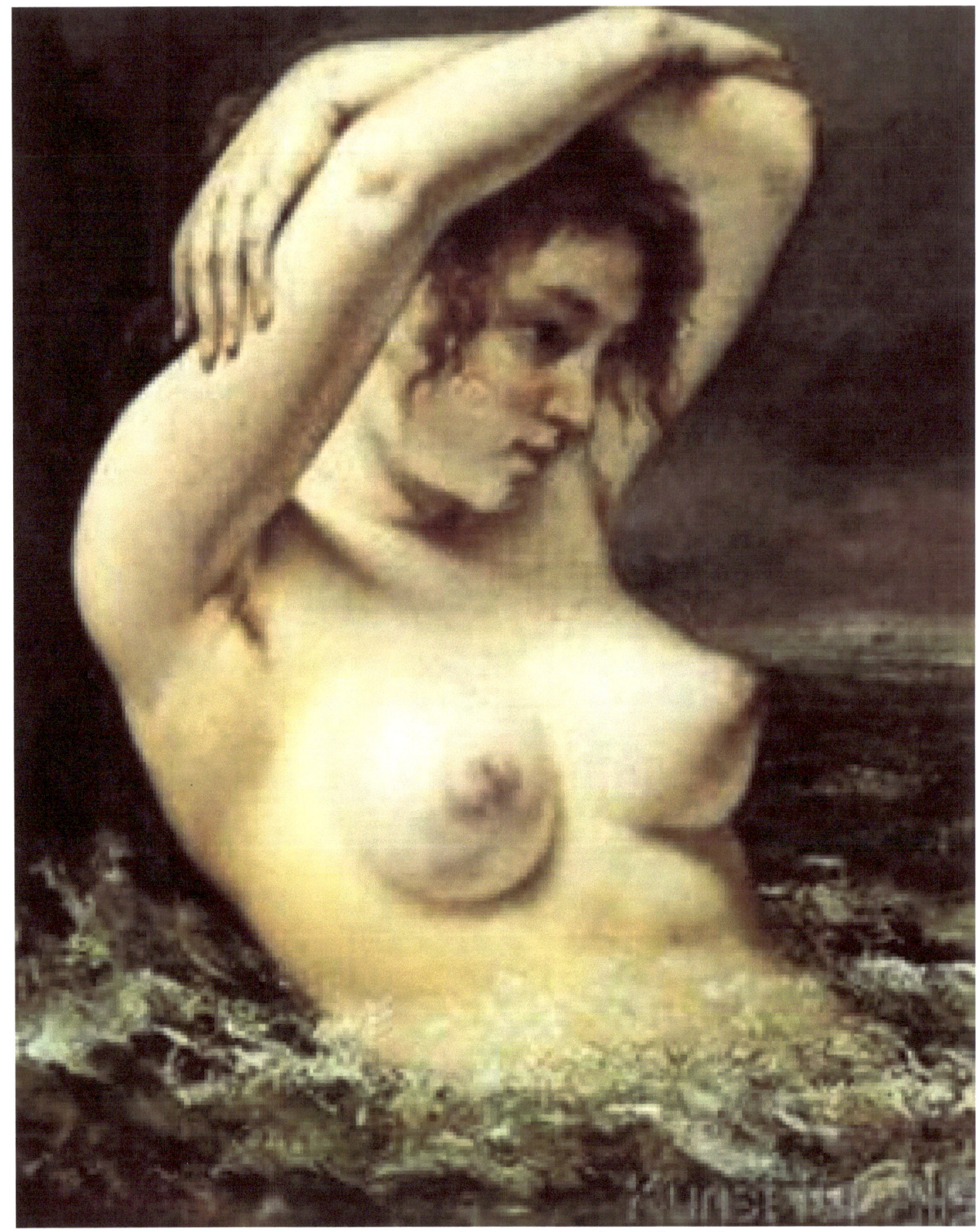

La femme a la vague – by Gustave Courbet, Year Unknown

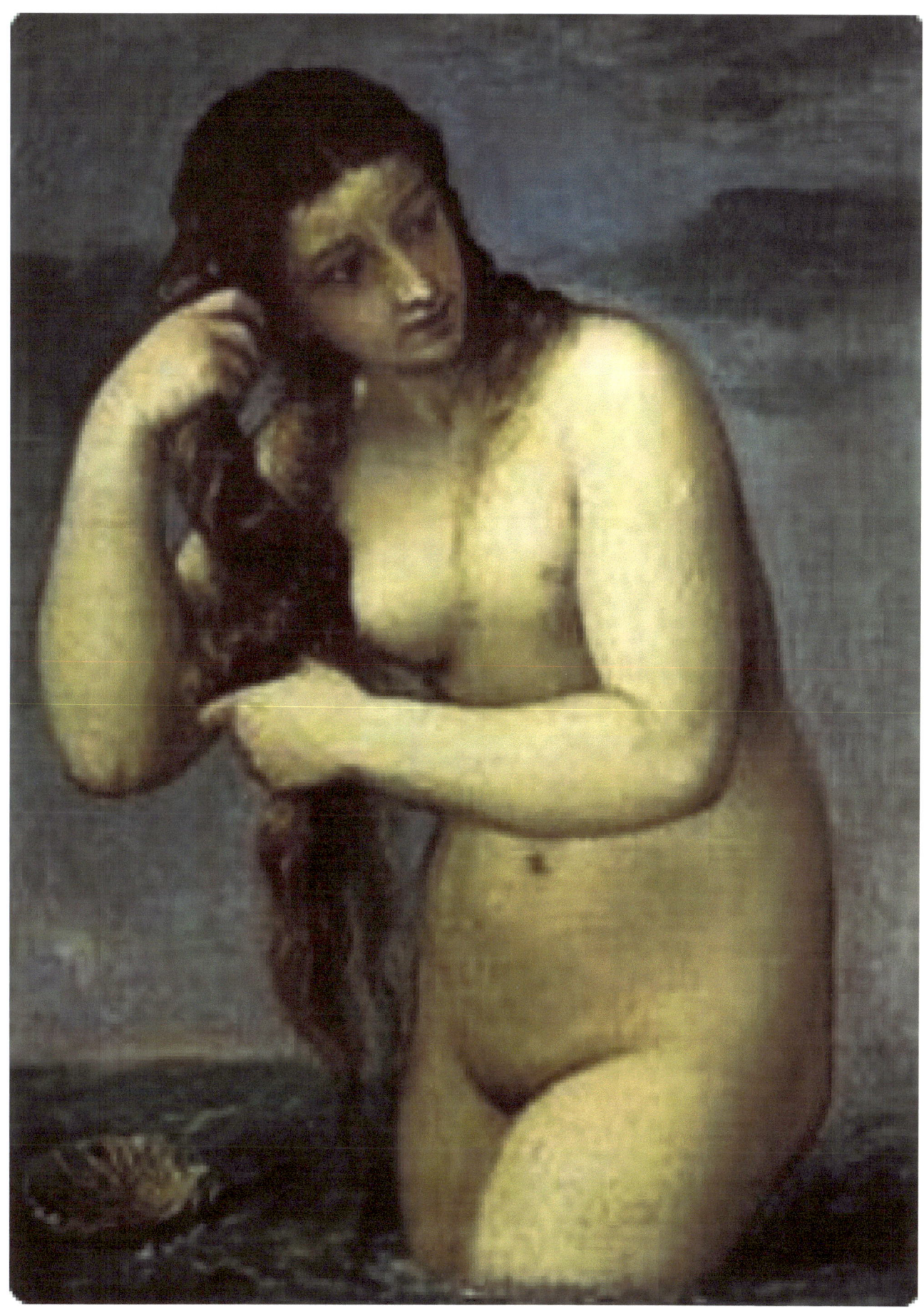

Venus Anadyomene, 1520 – by Tiziano Vecellio

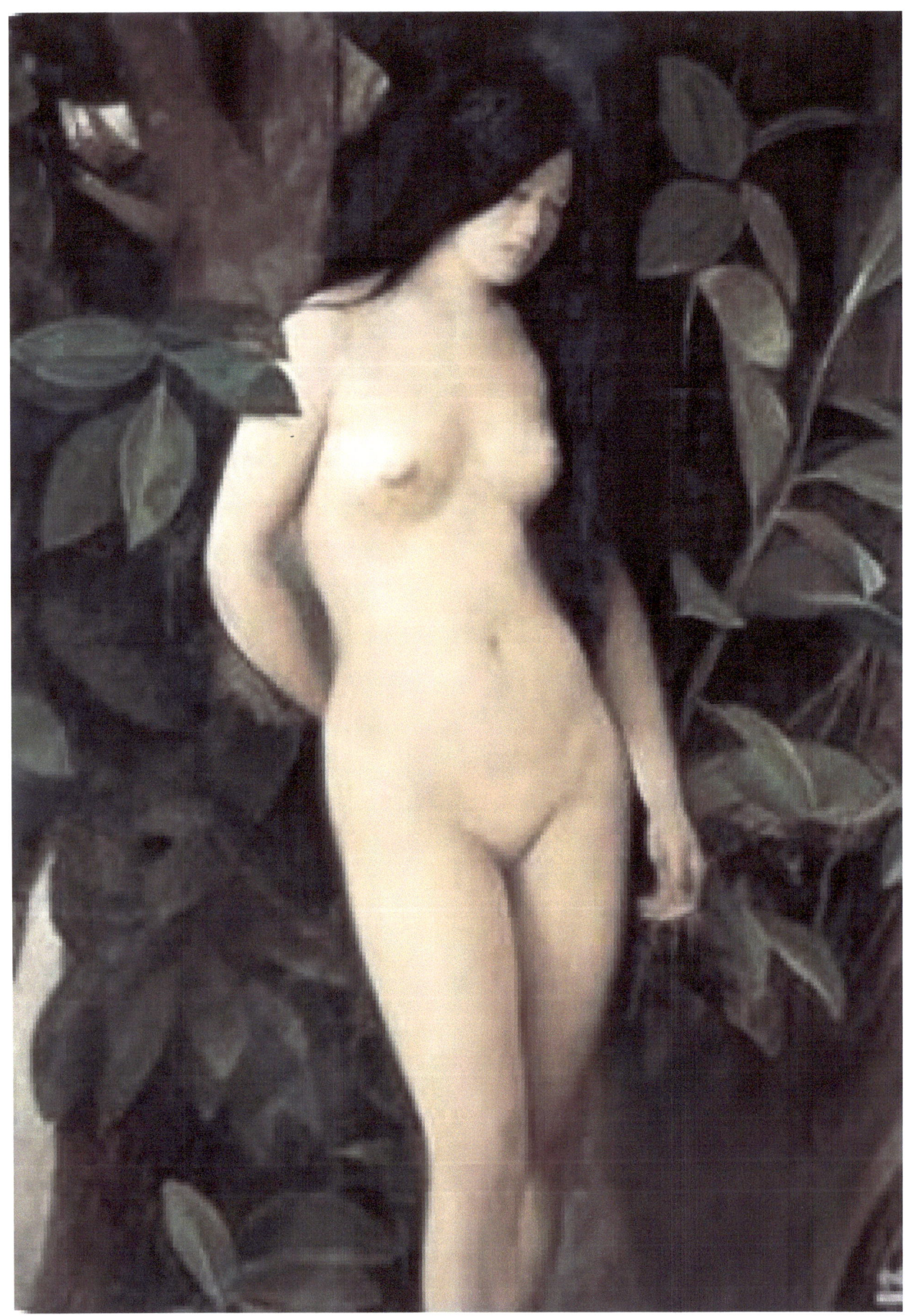

Chinese Artist, Li Xiaogang, Year Unknown

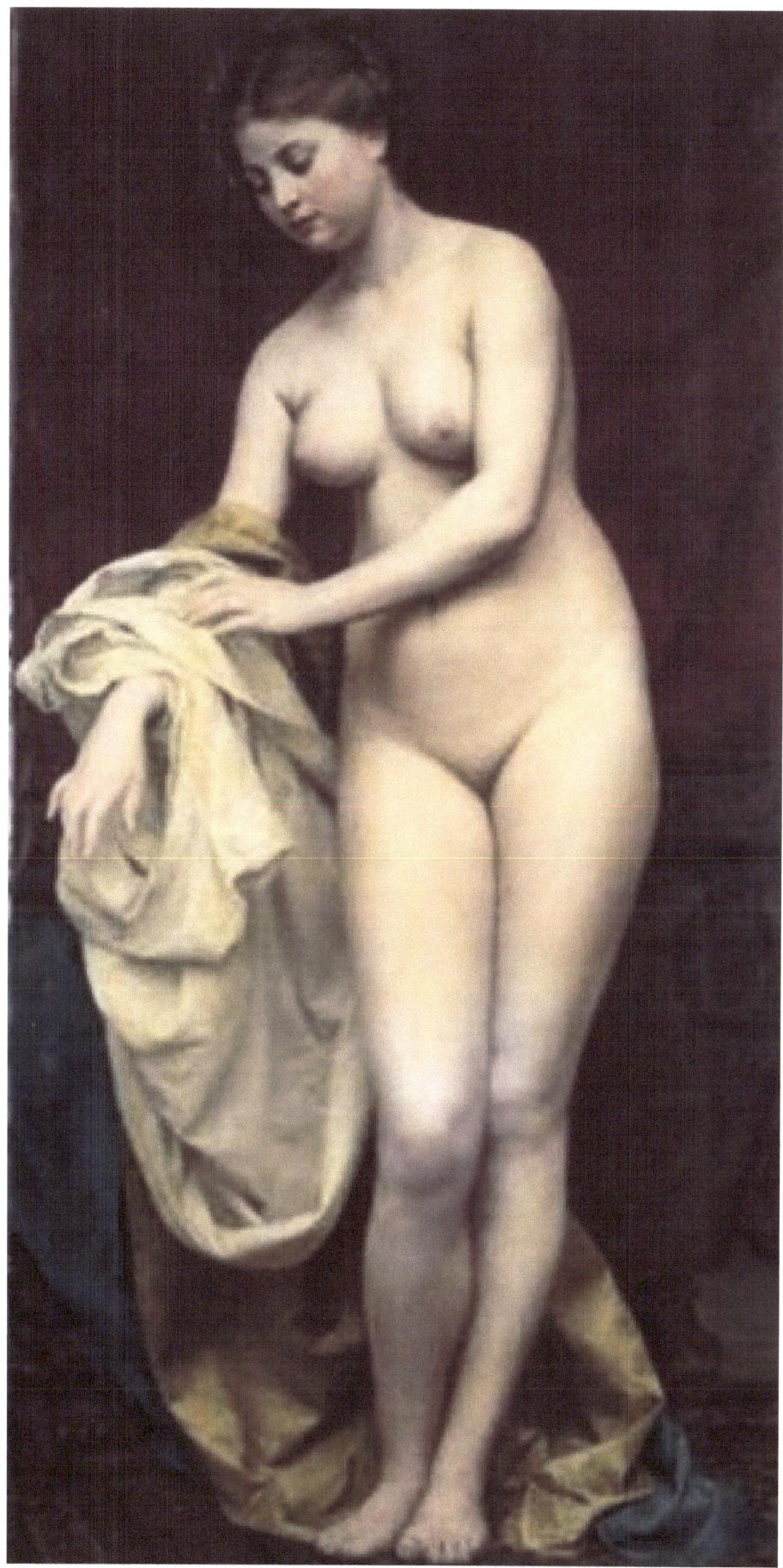

De Baadster - By Karel de Kessel, Year Unknown

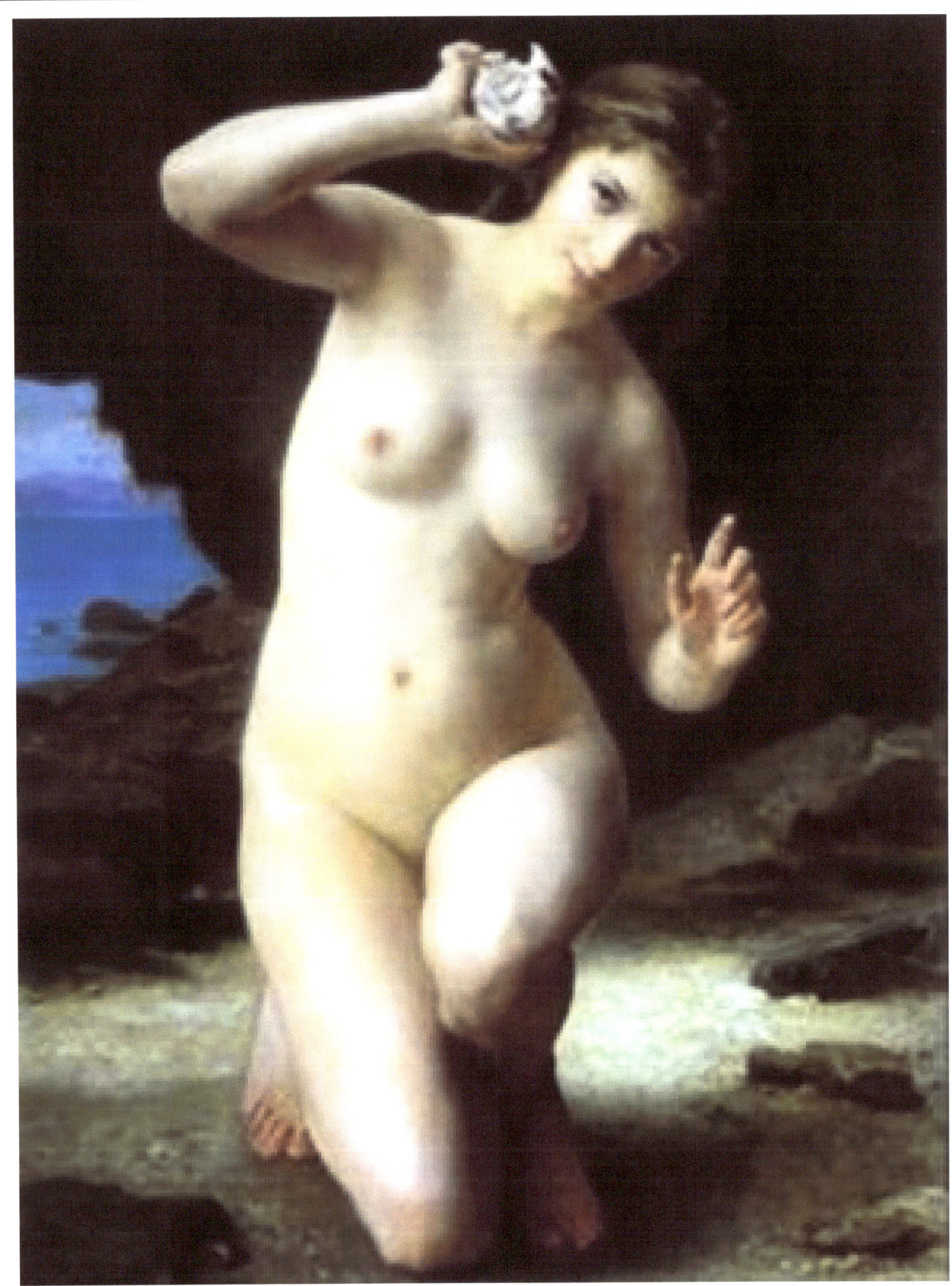

By William Adolphe Bouguerreau, Late 1800's

www.ingramcontent.com/pod-product-compliance
Lightning Source LLC
Chambersburg PA
CBHW051108180526
45172CB00002B/822